Marie-Pierre Colle

# Paraíso Mexicano

GARDENS, LANDSCAPES,
AND MEXICAN SOUL

INTRODUCTION BY
ALFONSO ALFARO

CLARKSON POTTER/PUBLISHERS
NEW YORK

Published by Clarkson Potter / Publishers, New York, New York.

Member of the Crown Publishing Group.

Random House, Inc. New York, Toronto, London, Sydney, Auckland.

www.randomhouse.com

CLARKSON N. POTTER is a trademark and POTTER and colophon are registered trademarks of Clarkson N. Potter, Inc.

Printed in China

Design by Julio Vega

Library of Congress Cataloging-in-Publication Data
Colle, Marie-Pierre.
Paraíso Mexicano: gardens, landscapes, and Mexican soul / Marie-Pierre Colle.—1st ed.
1. Gardens—Mexico. 2. Gardens—Mexico—Pictorial works. I. Title.
SB466.M6 C65 2002
712'.0972—dc21      2001035984

ISBN 0-609-60686-7

10 9 8 7 6 5 4 3 2 1

First Edition

PHOTO CREDITS APPEAR ON PAGE 240 AND CONSTITUTE AN EXTENSION OF THIS PAGE.

Photographers: Guillermo Aldana, Laura Cohen, Gabriel Figueroa Flores, Eric Giebeler, Amanda Holmes, Juan Pintor, Armando Salas Portugal, Bob Schalkwijk, Pim Schalkwijk, Ignacio Urquiza, Alejandra Villela

Translator: Andrea Dabrowski

Botanist: Juan Guzzy

Editorial Assistants: Miriam Arriaga Franco, Gracia Anguiano

Research Assistant: Mónica Hernández

PAGE 1: Gold barrel cactus and rabbit-ears, in the González Carbonel garden.

PAGES 2–3: Traveler's tree against the Mexican sky.

PAGE 4: Golden-trumpet frames a fountain in Punta Ixtapa.

OPPOSITE: A field of cockscomb in early November, around the Day of the Dead.

OVERLEAF: A window covered by ivy geranium in Bodegas del Molino.

## ACKNOWLEDGMENTS

It was thanks to Didier and Barbara Wirth, passionate gardeners, that I launched into the adventure of writing and producing this book. They own the famous seventeenth-century Brécy garden in Normandy and over the last decade have been restoring it to its original splendor.

I appreciate and thank my friend the art historian Alfonso Alfaro for his introduction. His sensitivity and knowledge are reflected in his text.

Juan Guzzy was of great help. He is a landscape architect with profound knowledge of botanical science. We spent many days together checking plants and studying them carefully, leaf by leaf, for this book. I have learned a lot from him. Paula Cussi was of great support, all along this project. I thank the owners of the gardens, too numerous to mention them all; in particular María Felix, Juan Soriano, Casa-Museo Luis Barragán, The Barragán Foundation in Germany, the government of the state of Jalisco, the Fundación de Arquitectura Taratia Luis Barragán, A.C., Lydia Sada, Adán and Bertha Lozano, Nicole Dugal, Casa de la Bola Museum, The Robert Brady Foundation, and the Franz Mayer Museum.

In the Foreign Affairs Office, I am particularly grateful to Ambassadors Roberta Lajous and Manuel Cosío.

My friends Aníbal and Mónica González, as well as Pilar de Patrón, took us to most of the haciendas in Yucatán and offered their wonderful hospitality.

I would also like to thank the owners of several marvelous gardens that, for lack of space, could not be included in the book.

My gratitude to AeroMéxico and in particular to Jean Berthelot. The photographers and I flew to many parts of the country that we would not have been able to reach without their generous help. His assistant, Anabel Reynoso, was most helpful.

My deepest thanks to architect Alberto Robledo, who knows the gardens of Veracruz so well. He significantly enriched our investigation as he took us to hidden gardens we would not have seen without him.

Architect and botanical expert Clio Capitanachi, of the Ecological Institute of Veracruz, and Rebeca Bouchez, from the Xalapa historical center, were most helpful.

I thank INBA (the National Institute of Fine Arts), INAH (the National Institute of Anthropology), and UNAM (the National University of Mexico) for their support.

I thank Guillermo Tovar y de Teresa for providing unique photographs of his family garden.

My deepest gratitude to Gracia Anguiano, who worked on the style correction of the edition in Spanish. She brought excellent suggestions to the text.

At the office, I thank the loyal and efficient editorial assistant for this book, Miriam Arriaga Franco, and the studious Mónica Hernández.

At home: Aurora García, Luisa Islas, and Rubén Barreto.

Photographers Guillermo Aldana, Laura Cohen, Gabriel Figueroa Flores, Eric Giebeler, Amanda Holmes, Juan Pintor, Armando Salas Portugal, Bob and Pim Schalkwijk, Ignacio Urquiza, and Alejandra Villela have done a great job. Their sensitivity can be felt, touched, and seen in every page of the book. Many thanks to all of them.

I have strongly felt the presence of my agent, Barbara Hogenson. During some difficult moments she was able to lead us to higher plateaus with this book.

Lic. José Luis Caballero Leal provided important advice.

This is the third book after *Casa Mexicana* and *Frida's Fiestas* with my editor at Clarkson Potter, Roy Finamore. I honor his professionalism and great interest in Mexico. Through these books he has really captured the essence of Mexican values. It is the second book I have done with Julio Vega, the designer. I admire his talent.

My deepest thanks to my friend and editor at Editorial Planeta, René Solís, and to his crew, Jesús Anaya, Margarita Sologuren, and Arlette de Alba.

I have had constant help from my family, in particular from Eric Giebeler, my son, and my sister, Béatrice Saalburg. She is herself a great gardener in Normandy. Their love has allowed me to walk through the paths of beauty in life.

And last, but not least, my deepest thanks to Dr. Alfonso Ricart Velazquez, who has helped me to cultivate my inner garden.

Tepotzotlán, March 2001

For Didier and Barbara Wirth, two passionate gardeners

# Contents

# Introduction

## The Gardener and the Cloud

Mexican gardeners have inherited secret powers: they can identify all the sounds of night and read the signs of dawn. Descendants of a people who, independent of Europe, discovered the art of agriculture, they belong to an ever-diminishing breed that knows the haunts of the wind and understands the dreams of water.

Many of the plants that these gardeners cultivate were first extracted from the wild by their forefathers, whose inventiveness and artistry changed them into sweeter, juicier, and far less savage species.

## The Realm of the Visible
## (Sky, Water, Earth, and Sea)

In Mexico the sun is proud, stubborn, unrelenting. The country's ancient inhabitants worshipped it in fear and trembling, moved by the stark contrast between daylight and the anxieties that nighttime brought. For them the sun was a generous but cruel deity that yearned for blood and sacrifice. The Mexican earth, too, feels the strongest of passions. Its precipices, canyons, and volcanoes weave a rugged design that was long ago given the crude and incongruous name of Sierra Madre. Extreme opposites of desert and jungle frame the features of a face that often forces the fertile, open plains into the background.

The same holds true for the waters of our region, which are not always placid. Rivers are rarely navigable, so riverbeds tend to be rocky and rugged. Through them flow trickles of water or mighty deluges: either silent streams waiting in the darkness of cenotes or torrents that plummet from great heights, filling the air with their roar.

Our national territory is enclosed by an endless, echoing coastline whose curves turn the waves into a broken line of nooks and crannies that are both private and open to infinity.

For country people there are only two seasons: dry and wet. Although they lack the violence of a monsoon, the rains arrive like an explosion, in a loud celebration that rumbles the air with lightning and peals of thunder. Gray skies and gentle, consistent humidity are familiar elements in the temperate zone. Here, halfway through a sunny day the air can become rudely charged. The intense blue suddenly turns violet and black, as the *tlaloques* (the Aztec spirits of water) move to embrace the needy earth. Children raise hands and faces toward the beneficent gift while men and women huddle underneath eaves of tile or thatch, seized by feelings of both dread and delight. The real rejoicing comes later, when the cloudburst is over and the air is freshened and the sky takes on the overblown, unreal hues that the children of this landscape

**PAGE 10:** Niña Susana de Teresa y de Teresa, floating like a fairy, the day of her first Communion, above the sublime Gelatti family garden located in the fashionable Tacubaya area, at the turn of the century.

**PAGES 12–13:** A panoramic view of the Gelatti garden with its lake, a Byzantine-style chapel in the center. Behind it, the train that used to go from one family garden to the other.

**OPPOSITE:** An allée of glossy privet (*Ligustrum lucidum*) leads to a gazebo, typical of the 19th-century French gardens.

try to capture in the color of their clothing, which is their legacy to art.

The plants (and people) that have most successfully adapted to this region are those that have managed to withstand and also benefit from a lifestyle of feast and famine, of long-suffered want broken by outbursts of unrestrained thanksgiving.

## Transparent Circles

MESOAMERICA. The ancient Mexicans were trapped in a circle of volcanoes and limited to a dialogue with the sun and the clouds. They placed their hopes in the soil and the firmament above, as well as in their own powers of invention. How were they to focus on serenity amidst such extravagant natural beauty? How could they create balance and continuity? In Mexico the sun seems all-powerful, time is impossible to grasp, and neither can be placated except through prayer, offerings, and sacrifices. Aside from the sun, there is only earth and water, elements with which the people of this land have spent dozens of centuries trying to strike a compromise.

In order to tame such an environment, people had to turn to plants. In the works upon which the native peoples founded their civilizations culture was synonymous with plant life, and plant life was transformed into art. This is where the hidden key to Mesoamerican civilization can be found, in its garden-terraces, canals, and *chinampas*.

The indigenous peoples claimed that the space inhabited by human beings was a flower floating on a surface of water, a flower with an enormous corolla consisting of four petals: red, black, white, and blue. At the center was a button of jade, its green an echo of the fire-god's home. They also said that the world rested on four trees that rose from the underworld toward the heavens: their roots plumbed the depths of darkness but their crowns were lost in the unseeable heights.

But nature had not made a gift of the most productive fields cultivated by the ancient civilizations. On the contrary, they were the fruit of hard work and clever planning. In order to distill drinking water from salt water the native lords designed dikes, which the common laborers built into a network of lagoons. Over the course of generations workers gradually built up platforms of cane and rush that they turned into *chinampas,* or floating gardens. Fertilized with mud and constantly exposed to water, these floating platforms were attached to the bottom of the lake by the willows that served as living anchors.

The floating gardens of Mexico are one of the most productive methods of intensive cultivation known to mankind, and quite possibly

Mesoamerica's most outstanding contribution to the history of technology. The network of canals was a refuge in a harsh land, a perennially blooming garden, and an inexhaustible showcase of plant life.

In those years the region produced what was perhaps the richest courtly society in its history. Even today there is stunning evidence of the splendor of its pleasure gardens, with their wonderful aromas, appealing colors, and the sumptuous baths called *temascales*. Everything came together here: the growing of crops, the great wealth that accrued principally to the ruler of the theocratic state, science based on botany and astronomy, medicine in the form of herbal science and magic (as in other agricultural civilizations), and an urban life centered on the lakes. In a world largely sustained by the mysterious cycles of plant life, gardening was the master art: the most life-giving store of wisdom resided in both the undeniable delicacy and the awesome resilience of plants.

In their way of seeing things and working with their hands, the people of the Mexican countryside still know how to decipher a language that was thousands of years in the making and can still tell spellbinding tales to those possessed of sufficient inner silence.

Despite the centuries that have passed since the collapse of those empires and the disappearance of their gods, robust remnants of a culture created by gardeners who worshipped the sun and the rain have

**ABOVE:** Barragán's Pedregal residential gardens, Mexico City. Designed by architect Luis Barragán between 1945 and 1950, this model garden was built in the lava rocks in Pedregal in the southern part of Mexico City. It became one of Barragán's most important urbanist projects. With the help of Chucho Reyes, Mathias Goeritz, and architect Max L. Cetto, he created elements that humanized the landscape. Today, only vestiges remain.

survived to this day. These places are still refuges where men and women can work together to natural rhythms that make each year resemble a liturgical cycle.

Where the continent narrows, out toward the coast of the turquoise sea, there are jungle kingdoms where one finds precious woods, silk-cotton trees, quetzal birds, and orchids. In such places water is often the supreme mystery: through the cenote, sacred precinct of life and death, mankind has a way to touch the dark and tragic world of the depths.

**DESERT AND OASIS.** Mesoamerica used to terminate at a vague and changeable frontier. To the north was the great continent of arid plains punctuated by oases. In them plants with heavy leaves and thorns as hard as steel had adapted to the drought and its rigors.

Although sun and silence were the sole rulers of those endless lands, they nevertheless witnessed the splendor of unfettered glory when the cacti displayed their fleeting luxuriance to a stunned audience of eagles, snakes, and coyotes, and the nomadic tribes that roamed the invisible wilderness paths. The cactus flowers—yellows, whites, and purples—burst and faded away to the metronome-beat of hidden seasons. Hunters and gatherers approached these flaming flowers with reverence and curiosity. In some of the plants, like peyote, shamans discovered gateways to worlds even more terrifying than the desert and its predators.

These oases are spread across enormous open spaces that the wars of the nineteenth century cut in half.

Like the sharp-edged shadows and naked rock, the magueys and the cactus, the gardens of desert and oasis are a gift given only to perceptive eyes, an offering made solely to those who value paradox and unprecedented beauty.

**THE VALLEY: SQUARE, CLOISTER, AND PATIO.** From Spain came peonies, oranges and almonds, cypresses, oaks, and jasmine. Their arrival changed forever the face of the sun, the soul of the water, and the moods of the land.

From the sixteenth century on nothing would be the same in Anáhuac. Even the inhabitants of the heavens began abandoning their dwellings, which eventually became homes for more forgiving gods, with faces more closely resembling our own. The new Mother of the land had sun-darkened skin, but the offering with which she sealed the covenant of blood with her new children was a cape made of simple peasant cloth covered with roses of Castile.

**ABOVE:** A view of the floating gardens of Xochimilco, famous since prehistoric times, and still very popular today.

One lake—Texcoco—soon entered its death throes, while another—Pátzcuaro—would be pushed to the side of new routes and transformed into a utopian refuge and laboratory for the meeting of civilizations. Horses, cattle, chickens, and sheep did their part to shape this much larger and more homogeneous territory and in the process help found the nation we know today.

When the civilization that had grown up around the lakes had finally been superseded and the terraced hillsides were dying, the day of the plains arrived. Plough and yoke became symbols of a natural order henceforth dominated by wheat and cattle (even maize would be adapted to European tools). A new civilization based on iron and gold took over from the old one, whose power grew from the peasant's hoe and whose splendor was measured in jade and quetzal feathers.

The land also emerged from its self-absorbed isolation. From that moment forward, Mexico joined the world. Incorporated into a cultural context of planetary dimensions, the natural landscape of Mexico was transformed. Its gardens received gifts from the lands of the mango and the clove, while cinnamon and tamarind arrived on galleons out of Manila. More than anything else, they made their own the heritage that the Greeks, Jews, Persians, Arabs, Byzantines, Flemish, and Tuscans had bequeathed to the Iberian Peninsula.

In the society of New Spain, plants were arranged by Mediterranean design, in squares, cloisters, and patios. Where American cities spread out horizontally from Main Street, the center of collective life in Mexico is the square, which pulls everything toward it. The square, descendant of the Greek agora, was home to robust plant species and luxuriant foliage. Sheltered by its benevolent shade, Mexicans learned how to communicate and get along with each other.

Because of the square, people learned their place on an imaginary map on which position, rank, and race were represented by concentric circles. There they also learned the auxiliary truth that desire is not governed by the spheres that set social hierarchies in motion.

From the middle of the sixteenth to the middle of the twentieth century, following Mass on Sunday and the Rosary on weekday afternoons, our fellow citizens enjoyed strolling through their city squares and village commons. Men circulated in one direction and women in the other, with growing fluency in the basic Mexican language of the furtive glance and unspoken dialogue. In this way the racial laws and rigid classifications that had been invented to imprison entire populations in a system of castes and privileges gradually lost their influence.

**ABOVE:** A florist sells her flowers from her *trajinera* (small boat).

From the sound of bandstand music and birdsong that enlivened even modest neighborhood gardens, to the squares of provincial capitals and the great central square of the Capital—the Zócalo—city squares provided a backdrop for young boys making gifts of flowers, sweets, and bottles of flower-water to girls who received them with an imperceptible thrill.

In squares (as in church gardens, on the sidewalk, or walking in procession) Mexicans learned to look one another in the eye and thereby come together. A mestizo nation came into being among the poplars, ashes, bay trees, and oaks.

THE CLOISTER. New Spain was one of the jewels in the Habsburg crown, a place where botany caught the interest of minds imbued with Renaissance enthusiasms and Baroque passion. A number of factors ensured that from the very beginning plants would be a matter of strategic importance to viceregal society. Among them were the need to explore and report on the status of the colonies through inventories of stock and accounts of unusual phenomena; an interest in pre-Hispanic societies that found expression in monumental ethnographic works composed by missionaries and chroniclers; and the mysteries and challenges represented by the healing properties of local plants.

These lines of research led to the writing of codices—each one of them a virtual garden that sought to reveal the secrets of folk medicine and decipher pictographic representations of native flora. One of these was written by Francisco Hernández, first physician to Philip II.

The monastic orders built their cloisters in imitation of the garden that traditionally represented Paradise. Cloisters were walled gardens of both faith and learning located at the heart of monasteries and universities. In them European science made the first systematic attempts to analyze and classify native plant life; it was there also that specimens collected by itinerant preachers and scholars first mingled with plants recently arrived from Spain. Dahlias and carnations came together in the cloister, and from cloisters maize and cocoa first found their way to Europe.

The cloister is related to the Roman villa, the curia, and the *cour*, from which are derived our notions of courtesy and etiquette. Like the city square, it is rectangular in shape, a place suited to the refinements of art and learning but essentially a center of devotion enclosed by high walls. Like Eden after the Fall, it opens only to the heavens.

Monastic gardens are created in honor of a reality that cannot be seen. Their arches frame broad vistas of sky and wind that evoke everything that surpasses the limits of sight: their builders knew well that what is truly important is not accessible to the eyes. Through these horizontal windows onto the infinite the eyes of the body can, through meditation, give us an oblique glimpse of everything that we cannot apprehend. This is the purpose of the cloister's four-sided fragment of sky: to put the worshipper's soul in touch, through the physical senses, with the scarcely guessed-at totality of creation.

Since the cloister is both natural paradise and garden of clouds, an ongoing dialogue takes place in the pool, fountain, or well located at its center.

The convent garden is intended to do more than put food on the table: as the only appropriate dwelling place for the eternal Word, it is a tool for strengthening inner peace and an instrument for creating perfect silence. This was the intention of the architects and workmen who erected these enormous structures that dot the Mexican landscape. Only a motivation of such magnitude can explain the majesty of buildings erected in defiance of time itself, and the dignified essence of gardens and orchards designed to be refuges of quiet for scientist and cleric alike.

Mexican houses are modeled after the houses of Seville, whose flower-filled hallways embrace airy courtyards awash in sunlight. Whether in the Viceroy's palace or the nobleman's mansion, the country estate or simple farmhouse, the palace or peasant home, in large areas of the country the Mediterranean patio was the vital standard of civil architecture. These two almost identical versions of the same spatial concept, the cloister and the patio, united different ethnic groups and social hierarchies under a common aesthetic, which was a shared understanding of the relationships between people and plants, earth and sky.

Square, cloister, and patio are the foundational spaces of our society, which still strives to foster the coherence of its peoples.

THE FRENCH GARDEN. As in all of the Spanish colonies, our country's destiny took an abrupt turn in the eighteenth century, though the changes were more superficial and less far-reaching than its proponents intended.

The spirit of the Enlightenment arrived in Madrid in the carriages of the new Bourbon dynasty. Suddenly there was a desire to change everything, from science to politics, and from working conditions to cultural life. This new world order, governed by dreams of openness and order, gave rise to a new way of thinking about flower growing. The new ideals were the parterre and the avenue.

Scientific exploration, which peaked in this period, also reflected this norm. With the emphasis on practicality, plants were less and less viewed as mysterious symbols. The Jardin des Plantes in Paris became the model on which our botanical gardens were based.

The new goal was to build spaces that answered to the dictates of pure reason and unflinching determination. The ideal was no longer the Garden of Eden but the field of Mars, Neptune's fountain, or Apollo's garden: not the eternal reality evoked by the fragments of sky that enclosed the original monastic garden at Monte Cassino, but the *tapis vert* of the Sun King's palace—the sweeping expanse visible from the windows of a building designed to glory in the pomp of earthly power.

The Gallery of Mirrors at Versailles is a theater of illusions that transforms the human gaze into pure self-referentiality, so that it can believe itself capable of ruling the palace and by extension the whole world.

In the New World only one city fell entirely under the spell of this rationalist dream. In L'Enfant's plans, Washington, D.C., aspired to be the world capital of the Enlightenment concept of space. Needless to say, such ambitions met with serious resistance in Mexico (what more eloquent sign of the cultural abyss that separates us from the United States?).

French taste did make itself felt nevertheless in many of our urban gardens, especially those of Chapultepec Castle and Reforma, the road that connected the Imperial residence to the city. Viceroys influenced by French taste had already given the city the Paseo de Bucareli and the new design of the Alameda.

This park was abandoned some decades ago by the city's elite, whose passion for the automobile disqualified them from the great urban privilege of walking. As a species they can no longer move without the artificial limb of the internal combustion engine. Happily, the residents of the old boroughs and recent immigrants from the country have claimed this elite space for themselves. By taking over the ruler-straight avenues that fan out in the shape of a star, as in Paris, they have transformed the Alameda into the largest village square on the continent and one of the most exuberant gardens in Mexico. Diego Rivera captured this bubbly vitality, no longer the meeting place of the city's rich but one of the most cherished of the capital's breathing spaces.

Every Sunday afternoon this urban area is taken over by young immigrants from the countryside and the provinces. The real nation is always stronger than efforts to make it conform to a rationalist's dream. The Bourbons were merely the first in a long but persistent line of frustrated modernizers.

**ANGLO-SAXON INFLUENCE.** As the centers of power changed, so did the ruling elites and their taste. The colonial nobility's aristocratic pretensions gave way to the nouveau riche passion for all things French, which in turn was superseded by the American dream of a middle class. Today's Mexico, which strives to adapt to freeways and skyscrapers, looks to the suburban lifestyle of mall and golf course for guidance in planning its cities.

The Scottish lawn's perpetual green, gift of the wet winds that con-

**ABOVE:** Malinalco convent, 17th century, Edo de Mexico. Detail of the fresco in the Agustinian cloister with flowers, fruits, and parrots of the region.

stantly rake that isolated land, has proven seductive for many Mexicans. It is not uncommon for today's gardeners to go to great lengths in an attempt to create smooth, gentle, undulating surfaces. With great effort they have succeeded in acclimatizing many grasses to even the most arid regions of Mexico. The power of fantasy holds even nature at bay.

Because, like other kinds of art, gardens are the product of willpower and imagination; they are often created against the dictates of logic or convenience. There are impeccable lawns in Mexico today in much the same way that French parterres were successfully planted in frozen St. Petersburg. Societies are constantly making mirrors in which to view the face they see in their dreams.

**ARTISTS' GARDENS.** Artists often walk a lonely road far distant from those trod by the majority of people. Their paths are determined by the most powerful of inner voices. If we bother to listen to them and follow their example, we may be startled at first, but if as spectators—or visitors to a garden—we allow ourselves to be touched by work born of rigorous faithfulness to an obsession, the payoff often exceeds our expectations.

**ABOVE:** Sunrise above a Tabasco landscape near the Usumacinta River. A silk-cotton tree *(Ceiba pentandra),* the sacred tree of the Maya, and a cohune palm *(Orbignya cohune).*

In Mexico there are many famous artists' gardens, defined as spaces conceived by passionately held aesthetic visions. One thinks of Edward James and Luis Barragán. Though contemporaries, they had completely opposing personalities and are therefore excellent examples of two very different adventures in search of nature's hidden face.

James created an implausible garden in the middle of a mountain jungle in Huasteca, a *folie* in which the dividing line between walls and plants is consciously blurred. This garden has the character of an elemental offering, a gratuitous act that draws equally on sculpture and gardening, and a point midway between daydream and nightmare.

A close cousin to Piranesi's flights of fancy, Xilitla is first and foremost an oneiric game, a garden of imagination. The ghosts of English Romanticism and French surrealism sigh and cackle in the dense green indigenous landscape, home of little smiling faces and the aroma of vanilla.

Luis Barragán is one of this country's greatest and most original artists. At the beginning of his career, his brilliant but unfashionable reworking of a powerful cultural heritage that had been overlooked or forgotten for two hundred years took the century by surprise. He translated the voice of rural Baroque Mexico into the artistic idiom of the present, combining clean lines and vivid colors to create architectural environments filled with light. These exist in perfect relation to his gardens, with their sense of wonder and balance and their freedom from overstatement and affectation. Both are inspired by a desire to create living spaces that provide for a little more than the simple, unthinking mediocrity that often fills our everyday lives. Barragán creates environments that nurture the deep serenity that signals an openness to transcendence.

In addition to the gardens of the Ciudad Universitaria and the Pierre Marqués Hotel in Acapulco, Barragán designed entire urban developments with names like Stone Gardens, Forest Gardens, and Woodlands. In the various houses he created in Tacubaya, water, sky, and plant life collaborate in the same celebration of intelligence and feeling that rejoices in the inner life.

What is perhaps the most daring of his contributions to the art of gardening as well as the most futuristic of his attempts to fuse architecture and nature is the roof garden of the house where he spent the last forty years of his life. In this space those accustomed to the formal challenges of the twenty-first century encounter a new variation on the *hortus conclusus*, a cloister and patio for future generations with walls that cut straight lines through the sky, shaping fields of clouds out of the ideal purity of the heavens.

**PUBLIC GARDEN, SECRET GARDEN.** It is not surprising that the inhabitants of a country as varied as this have such different ways of relating to the natural world. In a fragmented society, where there are few areas for different kinds of people to mix and the interests common to all are given such tenuous expression, it stands to reason that most of the best gardens are private. Many of them aspire to understatement, like the magnificent natural compositions that transform mansions built on the edge of cliffs into paradises suspended between sea and sky.

A country's gardening and horticulture cannot be divorced from its inhabitants' relationships with one another. Plants reveal the state of the society that cares for them: countries that produce good gardens tend to have robust agriculture, coherent urban life, and a high level of cooperation among their citizens.

The upheavals of Mexican history led its ruling elite to turn its back on the rural world three generations ago, with visible consequences to our gardens, which internalize the tensions that afflict the rest of society. A country with ailing agriculture, chaotic urban life, and stressed lines of communication between its peoples can hardly be expected to have the cultural infrastructure required to maintain great public gardens. All the more remarkable, then, are the efforts of the current patrons of flower growing and horticulture who go against the status quo.

The unusual quality of many Mexican gardens sets them apart from an unfavorable social context. The majority of works of art depicted here are in fact truly gardens in the desert.

**MEMORY AND TIME TO COME.** What are the most promising points of contact—the closest ties—between the Mexicans of today and the realm of nature?

Two items symbolize this deep, seasoned, and still vibrant relationship: the *calmil* and the altar of the dead.

The *calmil* is a small seedbed (in its simplest form it may consist of nothing more than a few flowerpots). Aromatics, herbal teas, a few simple flowers, and maybe a few shoots of green corn grow in it, often without apparent order, in the absence of a nurturing environment. In the *calmil* peasant families and urban households that have not lost their vital connection with the sun and rain enter into a dialogue with the same soil out of which their own bodies were once formed.

These little nooks preserve the knowledge and feelings required to maintain any portion of the global surface with the vitality of a living tree. In this the *calmil* is no different from the most luxurious formal gardens, milpas, high-tech farms, or botanical laboratories. On the day our country awakens from its daydream of modernization through manufacturing and the service industries to the virtual exclusion of everything else, the day it remembers that the earth can love and breathe and show gratitude—on that day this knowledge will be put effectively to use.

**THE ALTAR OF THE DEAD.** The domestication of wild maize was the man-made miracle that gave birth to the civilizations of Mesoamerica. In North America, ears of corn are still a symbol of productive gardening. Thanksgiving, the most important family holiday in the United States, is directly linked to the corn cycle. The most important Native American ceremony south of the Río Bravo is likewise dependent on the corn cycle: the great banquet in honor of dead ancestors that is held at harvest time, in November. They are the recipients of the earth's most sublime gifts: flora and fauna, water and fire, wax candles and resin incense, all harvested thanks to the gardener's creativity and hard work. They symbolize the ancient covenant between mankind and nature, a covenant that the gardeners of this planet (sometimes also called peasants) renew daily.

A road of yellow cempazúchitl flowers identifies the route that the souls of the blessed must follow in order to reach the table where food offerings are carefully arranged so as to please the senses of the beloved dead. Their incorporeal eyes, their ethereal senses of smell and touch, and their supernatural palates take note of all the love that has gone into the preparation of these delicacies. They delight in the color and scent of the flower bouquets, and their disembodied hearing enjoys the harmonies of good feeling and affectionate words.

The altar of the dead is a sculptural composition featuring yellows and oranges, whites, mauve and cherry (colors of flowers and fruit). It is a living stage of mandarin oranges, tejocotes, sugarcane, and squashes. In this short-lived garden whose paths have been made to converge for the meeting of the living and dead, and that disappears when the candles are extinguished, families renew ties in a memorial thousands of years old.

Alfonso Alfaro

**OVERLEAF:** Hernán Cortés house, Antigua, Veracruz, built in the 16th century after the Andaluz style. It is said that the conqueror lived in this 22-bedroom house upon his arrival in the New World. Now, breathtaking Amates (*Ficus tecolutensis*) have taken over the walls, embracing the house in a mysterious, junglelike look. Nature may build as well as destroy a place.

## CHAPTER I

# The Mexican Landscape

According to the philosopher Francis Bacon, "The garden is the highest art form in any civilization. It is eternal like nature and changeful as a landscape."

"What a joy it is to walk in a garden! Like walking around the infinite," Kang-hsi rejoiced.

The great Mexican architect Luis Barragán said, "In the garden, the architect invites the plant world to collaborate with him. A beautiful garden is nature in all its permanence—nature reduced to human size and made to serve mankind. It is our best shelter against the violence of today's world."

Similarly, the French writer Ferdinand Bac tells us that the garden's soul encompasses the greatest amount of serenity available to mankind, since gardens hold the entire universe within them.

It is remarkable how many important figures throughout history have pondered on the garden and its significance, reaching the conclusion that a garden is nothing less than Paradise.

*Paraíso Mexicano* was born of a deep desire to share the essence of Mexico through its flora, its lush natural life, and its gardens. In presenting this book, there is no intention to compete with French, English, or Italian gardens. In Mexico, the entire landscape is a garden, as can be seen, for example, in the wonderfully evocative photographs of the Sonoran Desert, which blooms but once every sixteen years, or when the rain miraculously falls.

The ancient Mexicans cultivated what were probably the first botanical gardens in the world. Fifteenth-century Mexican gardens were usually located on mountain slopes near sources of water, as at Oaxtepec, Chapultepec, and Texcutzingo (similar "mountain gardens" were developed in Babylonia, China, and India). Hydraulic systems carried the water downhill through a series of terraces like the *chinampas* in the inland lakes at Iztapalapa, Xochimilco, and Tenochtitlán, where irrigation was easily provided.

With what delight the Spanish first beheld the gardens of Moctezuma and Netzahualcóyotl! The discovery of these gardens may well have been what spurred the creation of those same gardens in Europe, at the beginning of the sixteenth century. Cervantes de Salazar remarked that few princes, or maybe none, had ever possessed a pleasure garden equal to that of the great lord Moctezuma. Located in Oaxtepec, Morelos, they were nearly two leagues (five miles) in circumference. The gardens of the ancient palaces at Tenochtitlán were equally amazing. The palaces sometimes featured flower arrangements that were gardens in

themselves, floating down in the *chinampas* of Xochimilco. The Acolhua king Netzahualcóyotl had similar gardens at Texcutzingo, his famous palace in Texcoco.

Mexico's geological past accounts for the great variety of its terrain. Its complex topography includes coastal plains, canyons, highlands, plateaus, and enormous mountain ranges. Virtually all of the climates known to science are found in Mexico's broad biological spectrum, from the temperate, cold, hot, dry, and wet to an almost infinite range of microclimates. In the high mountains there are alpine meadows, and coniferous and mixed forests. At lower altitudes one finds a large variety of prickly, semiarid scrub forests; high-, medium-, and low-altitude jungles; grazing lands and pasturage; rows of coastal palms, mangrove swamps, and aquatic vegetation; and many other kinds of natural formations and vegetation. All of them contain a surprising variety of plants and animals that have been assimilated into the lifestyles of numerous ethnic groups.

**ABOVE LEFT:** Flowering green ebony (*Jacaranda mimosifolia*) in Tepotzotlán, Morelos.

**TOP:** A red cedar covered with epiphytes (*Tillandsia* spp.), at the cloud forest between Coatepec and Xalapa, Veracruz.

**ABOVE:** A field of blue agave (*Agave angustifolia*)—source of mezcal—in Oaxaca.

**OPPOSITE:** Wild lupine (*Lupinus polyphyllus*) at the Paso de Cortés seen from Puebla looking toward the Ixtaccíhuatl volcano.

1

2

3

5

4

1. A cactus barrel (*Echinocactus* sp.) in bloom.

2. The Sonoran Desert in bloom, covered with a creeping sand verbena (*Abronia* sp.).

3. A sahuaro (*Carnegiea gigantea*) at sunset in the Sonoran Desert.

4. A view of the desert near Guaymas, covered with ruderal plants. In the foreground is a prickly poppy (*Argemone platyceras*).

5. A poetic crown of evening primrose (*Oenothera californica*) has been formed by the winds on the desert sand.

**ABOVE:** A microphyll shrub formation at the national park of El Pinacate near the Altar Desert of Sonora.

Because Mexico is long and narrow, a geographically varied bridge between North and South America, its plant life is unusually exuberant. The sea has an important effect on the Mexican landscape, especially in the summer, when the humid east winds arrive to freshen large portions of the countryside.

There are thought to be more than 25,000 species of vascular plants in Mexico, which account for approximately 10 percent of the species on earth. This number surpasses the United States and Canada, which together have around 18,000 species, and is double the number for Europe.

According to the renowned Mexican botanists Faustino Miranda and Efraín Hernández Xolocotzi, there are 32 major types of vegetation in our country, between 1,000 and 1,100 species of ferns, and no fewer than 85 species of palm trees. The 50 varieties of pine trees in Mexico make up half of the known varieties in the world. This lush abundance is due to the tropical climate, as in Colombia, Brazil, and India.

Most important among other plants, the world owes to Mexico the dahlia (the country's national flower), begonias, poinsettias, avocados, tomatoes, tuberose, orchids, and cacti.

Our idea of a garden goes beyond the simple definition of a fertile, cultivated plot of soil. The Mexican garden can be found inside a volcano in Sonora or in the beautiful *chinampas* of Xochimilco, which have been called "floating gardens" since the ninth century. Mexico is the pre-Hispanic garden of the Chapultepec Forest, built for the emperor's pleasure and home to birds from all over the country. It is the Alameda, the first public park in the Americas, and the pantheon of the Day of the Dead, and the rose-and-gray parterre dreamt by the painter Francisco Toledo for the Convent of San Francisco in Oaxaca. It is the contemporary patio built around Teodoro González de León's pool and the disturbing surrealist garden that Edward James designed in the Huasteca Potosina, where he settled so he could hear the parrots sing. It is the mysterious green garden where architect Luis Barragán planted a pep-

**TOP:** On the road between Puebla and Oaxaca, a semiarid landscape with agave (*Agave* sp.) and sotol (*Dasylirion acrotriche*).

**ABOVE:** A succulent ground cover (*Sedum* sp.) grows in arid, sunny climates.

TOP: A yellow orchid (*Lycaste* sp.).

ABOVE: A hidden colonial church in the forest of Malinalco during the rainy season.

ABOVE RIGHT: A sea of ferns in the cloud forest near Cuetzalan, Puebla.

OVERLEAF: Sunset at the national park of Lagunas de Chacahua, Oaxaca, through a red mangrove screen (*Rhizophora mangle*).

per tree, so that its shadow would be projected on the nearby yellow wall, and it is the flower market at San Angel, or a gardenia pool in Fortín de las Flores (which means "the little fortress of the flowers").

Gardens are celebrations of the ephemeral, and yet they live on, changing from season to season. Fountains run dry, flowers wither, trees drop their leaves and eventually die, but as the great Argentine writer Jorge Luis Borges remarked, "As long as there is death, there is hope." After winter comes spring.

This book invites you to touch and feel our gardens, to listen to the grand symphony played by grasshoppers and frogs, insects and winds. According to André Breton, Mexico is where surrealism was born. Thereby, Mexico has the seed and the knowledge of the existing tension between chaos and order—that which is found at the heart of all things.

## CHAPTER II

The Popular Garden

**PAGE 44:** A little garden of marigold planted in the patio of Doña Martha in Santa Ana Segache, Ocotlán, Oaxaca.

**PAGES 46–47:** Orchids grow in cans and pots, hanging at the door of a humble house in Coatepec, Veracruz. This is typical of the popular garden all over Mexico. The essence is what matters, not the container.

**OPPOSITE TOP:** A little house in Puebla surrounded with florist's chrysanthemum, wild dahlias, and beggar-ticks.

**OPPOSITE BOTTOM LEFT:** A cactus wall (*Stenocereus marginatus*) tied with bamboo is often found in villages of Oaxaca and central Mexico.

**OPPOSITE BOTTOM RIGHT:** A stone arch opens on a garden filled with banana trees (*Musa platanus*), Abyssinian banana (*Ensete ventricosum*), croton (*Codiaeum variegatum*), coralblow (*Russelia equisetiformis*), and garland flower (*Hedychium coronarium*).

**ABOVE:** A woven bamboo fence covered with a passionflower vine.

The popular garden is a fertile land meant to show, to oneself and to others, that one has the power to do things, that one knows. It is a place of enchantment where we may recover from illness. "We must cultivate our garden," said the French thinker Voltaire. This idea of his has become one of the most popular and powerful in our culture.

By definition, the popular garden is eclectic; it projects immense poetry.

"My garden is not my garden when the parrot doesn't sing," my friend Memo Sepúlveda told me when I visited his garden, which has been left in a state of sophisticated abandonment. The generous disorder that seems to invade it is just one more facet of the creativity of Monterrey's famous gallery owner. He collects various objects of Mexican art, and he also manages to bring together families of succulents, rosebushes, and fruit and palm trees. The concept of collection is one of the characteristics of the Mexican popular garden.

All of us have childhood memories of our grandparents' gardens. Their mysterious force stays with us our whole lives. We remember the magnolia trees we used to climb, the scent of jasmine, the pots where we would hide some treasures, the tree that we planted so easily. In the garden we become mimics: we grow, just as the trees do, at the seasons' rhythm and we are born again into this fountain of life. "The tree gives you courage and strength," my grandmother would insist on saying whenever I was sad or tired. "Put your arms around it and tell him your problems. He will listen. Breathe in the pure and fresh breath of its leaves. Caress them. They will respond. They will move at the pace of your heartbeat."

The popular garden not only has flower trees and ornamental plants, but also spices for seasoning and medicinal plants. Clay pots cover the stone bench built against a wall, while low, built-in walls come together in the balconies, at the edge of a window, framing the house's main door. They hold the flowers and plants that, according to the indigenous tradition, are necessary to protect the home and the family's health. There is sweet basil to counter bad luck; rue for stomachaches and to get rid of the bad humor of those who are ill; aloe for good luck, which, as a mask, reduces the inflammation caused by mumps; oregano for happiness; yellow chrysanthemums, which attract money; the *axihuatl* that cures diabetes and heals wounds; and the lemon tea that cures all ills. Teas made from the little black hair that grows on corn cure inflammation. Corn leaves can be used to serve rice with milk on holidays; the bitter orange goes well with it, and makes the flavor of the fruit punch

1

2

1. Most Mexican is the adobe façade covered with ivy geraniums growing in cans. The house may be humble, but it is made joyful with its plants.

2. Detail of a popular garden with medicinal plants and flowers for the house. A Mexican bush sage *(Salvia leucantha)* is in the center.

3. In Yucatán, a typical Mayan hut with its wall covered with ciboule *(Allium fistulosum)* and herb teas growing in pots near the hibiscus *(Hibiscus rosa-sinensis).*

4. The adobe walls of this hut in Tlayacapan, Morelos, become a garden.

5. An enclosed kitchen garden behind a stone wall with very Mexican elements: dahlias *(Dahlia pinnata),* corn *(Zea mays),* and prickly pear *(Opuntia* sp.).

3

4

5

7

6

6. Doña Martha in her kitchen garden in Santa Ana Segache, Oaxaca.

7. A *terrasse* with potted orchids and bougainvillea in Coatepec, Veracruz.

much richer. Mammee, sapodilla or marmalade tree, medlar fruit, chayote *(Sechium edule)*: their leaves are good for the kidneys. We eat pumpkins, beans, and corn; all these grow side by side. The garden, as has been said already, is the union between man and the world we live in.

Multicolored bougainvillea cover the fences, forming impenetrable, ornate walls. In Oaxaca, the fences are made of woven ditch reeds dotted with organ cactus and prickly pears. In Huamantla, Puebla, the streets become tapestries covered with flowers, seeds, stones, petals, and sand in order to celebrate the Virgin's feasts.

From ancient times we have inherited a magnificent tradition: planting all around the walls of the house. In Mexican villages, the home's entire façade is a garden.

In Pochutla, Oaxaca, you need only reach out and the fruit is there, in the palm of your hand. This bonanza is repeated throughout the humid and tropical regions: plants grow practically on their own in their abundant natural surroundings. Imagine my surprise when we decided to enclose our little land in Tepotzotlán and I saw, soon after, that the fence posts that separated it from that of our neighbors had turned into luxuriant Indian laurel *(Ficus retusa)*. "The garden loves me; therefore, it has to obey me," said Trini, my gardener. "Sometimes the garden does not want us to visit. I know when the plants are sad and when they feel at ease."

To sit in one's own little garden and feel the evening dew is another way to experience the passing of time. Some gardens, in their simplicity, come closer to the world of emotion, touching us beyond words—more so than those gardens that are elaborate. I am thinking of the gardens we discovered in Oaxaca, in Yucatán, in Veracruz. The cycles of germination and growth are ever present: one feels the repose and the dreams that lie beneath them—the sunny, rainy, and cold seasons.

We share the voice of Carlos Pellicer, the Mexican poet, who says: "Something in me moves to the pace of the chlorophyll."

**OPPOSITE TOP:** A field of marigolds in the fall, the time of the celebration of the Day of the Dead in San Martín Texmelucan, Cholula, Puebla.

**OPPOSITE BOTTOM:** Families have decorated the tombs of loved ones in Cuetzalan, Puebla.

**ABOVE:** Flowers hang from a tree, a Mexican tradition to remember the loved one who died on the road.

**OVERLEAF:** Sunrise on the Day of the Dead under the Popocatepetl volcano in Calpan, Puebla.

# The Colonial Garden

In ancient Greece and Rome gardens had a sacred purpose. We have learned that they were enclosed spaces and that plants were chosen in terms of their symbolism. We presume, therefore, that ancient gardens were built according to specific standards derived from a ritual, and that their main trait was a geometric design.

The colonial garden, derived from the classical one, and in accordance with *Los Jardines en la Nueva España* by Don Manuel Romero de Terreros, is divided into civilian and monastic. After the Conquest, the Spaniards became known for the large residences they built: the country or pleasure homes owned by Hernán Cortés and others such as Cantabrana, in the suburbs of the great Tenochtitlán, and La Tlaxpana, "where elegance was squandered on its large orchards and gardens."

An important objective of the era was to subdue and conquer nature. It is possible that the colonial garden had luxuriant trees, meadows decorated with groups of herbaceous plants, flower baskets, mosaics, paths, various ornamental structures and water flowing in fountains, artificial streams and small ponds, to fit every taste and climate.

We are told that the Mexican courtyard, an outstanding part of the colonial garden, was born during this time. It was an inheritance of the *mestizaje* (the crossbreeding of the Spanish and Indian races), capable of transforming an entire space. It is a meeting point, a symbol of the community and the urban convergence of the four cardinal points. With its characteristic central fountain wholly covered by glazed tiles from Puebla or a stone quarry, the courtyard is planted with trees, including fruit trees—in the Castilian manner—to protect from the scorching sun.

The owner of the colonial garden understood the significance of having a garden and devoting himself to cultivating his land. This is how the ornamental plants made their grand entry, with their different forms, dimensions, and perfumes. They provided an enjoyable aesthetic setting, where the gardener's creativity and the clergyman's practical nature became evident.

"If viewed from above, the entire garden may be seen as an immense Talavera tile, due to its perfect design and symmetry," according to Romero de Terreros.

The taste for gardens and parks in the English, French, and Italian styles was rediscovered toward the end of the nineteenth century, following the Wars of Independence and Reform, when residents returned to their properties and were able to enjoy the European influence in the Porfiriato, as the reign of Porfirio Díaz is known.

## OAXACAN COLONIAL PATIO

The patio in this eighteenth-century colonial home springs from Oaxaca's traditional architecture, built after the construction of the outside aqueduct that brought the water from San Felipe del Agua to the city of Oaxaca.

This patio is the soul of the house—a particularly perfect space, with all the arcades and balconies from the house's two floors looking out on it.

Two blind walls are covered with jasmine and enclose the patio. These vines bestow a sense of freshness and greenery despite the reduced space. The bougainvillea are outstanding. In the lower part, we can see small annatto trees *(Bixa orellana)* blooming, in rose- and white-colored clusters. We find a wide variety of low bushes such as the guava and the pomegranate and potted elephant's-ear plants (a gift from the artist Francisco Toledo).

We also find rigid leaves in terra-cotta pots, gardenias, and other *nieva en París* bushes and poinsettias, with a bright red color for winter. On the upper floor there are potted geraniums, begonias, and crown-of-thorns with long, spiny branches; when these bloom, the flower is an intense red.

**OPPOSITE:** The arches and balconies are covered with jasmine and bougainvillea.

**TOP:** Storksbill bloom in pots from Oaxaca.

**ABOVE:** Palm-Beach-bells in an old terra-cotta pot.

**ABOVE RIGHT:** Pots on the colonial banister are filled with different seasonal flowers.

## LAS BODEGAS DEL MOLINO

**OPPOSITE:** The "President's fountain," a gift to President Avila Camacho, is from Puebla. Around it, a boxwood hedge (*Buxus sempervirens*).

**ABOVE:** Detail of a Byzantine pavilion, a 19th-century *folie* brought from Istanbul. In the pot, a dietes lily (*Dietes vegeta*); on top, an avocado (*Persea americana*).

**ABOVE RIGHT:** A stone stairway decorated with pineapples painted in old gold and copper with turquoise, which give the romantic feeling of the 19th century. Winged sphinxes, dolphins, Harpies, and Greek vases are also part of the décor.

**OVERLEAF:** The round fountain with a view toward the mill, framed by roses, boxwood, California privet, Abyssinian banana, and orange trees.

This remodeled building belongs to Roberto Trawitz and is the site of one of the best restaurants in Puebla—romantic, with a strong flavor of Porfirian and industrial times. Enrico Caruso sang in these gardens.

The back garden has a central fountain that once belonged to President Avila Camacho; a bronze eagle decorates it. Dolphins, Greek vases, and monstrous figures adorn the stairs and columns in the garden where pink angel's-trumpets (*Brugmansia arborea*), privet (*Ligustrum vulgare*), loquat (*Eriobotrya japonica*), walnut (*Juglans pyriformis*), and pomegranate (*Punica granatum*) grow.

Besides the President's fountain there is the Moghul fountain, which was brought from India, and the Lion's fountain, located in one of the patios.

## CASA DE LA BOLA MUSEUM

This eighteenth-century residence has been turned into a museum. Don Antonio Haghenbeck y de la Lama bequeathed it to the Mexican people.

Haghenbeck provided the romantic character of a nineteenth-century Baroque garden in the Italian style by placing stone and metal sculptures —such as the lions near the staircase to the house—around a marble fountain. Muses, in the Greek and Roman tradition, are scattered through the park, playfully descending upon us unexpectedly.

Today this eclectic garden comprises a wide variety of trees and plants: privet, green ebony, butterfly bushes, ash trees, eucalyptus, and cedar. Some paths made of volcanic rock, others of brick, allow us to approach the yuccas, the Abyssinian banana trees, the arborescent ferns, and the windowleaves. Among the flower plants we can admire are acacias, magnolias, camellias, eugenias, calla lilies, Indian-shots, heliconias, honeysuckle, lady's-eardrops, and lilies.

Due to the extravagance of nature, even in winter, some fruit trees— the sapodilla, or marmalade, tree, the cherimolas, the loquat trees, and mulberries—are green.

**OPPOSITE:** The romantic leafy garden, with Greek acanthus and cabbage trees seen through French gates.

**TOP:** The hexagonal Italian fountain adorns the southern façade.

**ABOVE:** A cabbage tree in front of a marble sculpture.

**ABOVE RIGHT:** Brick paths form a geometric design around the central fountain.

## EX-CONVENTO TLATELOLCO S.R.E.

Tlatelolco is, in a manner of speaking, where New Spain began, for it is on this site that the Aztec empire was defeated by Cortés.

The original convent was built a few years after the Conquest, near 1536. The Imperial College of the Santa Cruz—the first in America—had its downfall at the start of the seventeenth century; later, this new cloister and the Church of Santiago Tlatelolco were built in order to have a school for the Franciscan order. It is now home to the Ministry of Foreign Affairs.

From what was originally the Santa Cruz Convent, only the western façade remains. The seventeenth-century design of the convent's garden was kept, with all of its fruit trees—oranges, lemons, pears, mandarins, and nuts—that once provided food for the Franciscans.

The fountain, in the central part of the patio, preserves the seventeenth-century style. Four parterres still keep the free, cellular design with flowers: violets *(Viola odorata)* and geraniums *(Pelargonium peltatum)* from the seventeenth century were donated by the National Federation of Gardening. Roses with eight petals, others with eleven, stand out from the current classical roses.

**OPPOSITE:** Seville orange trees, mandarin orange, cherry plum, pear, walnut, coffee, and a boxwood hedge grow around the fountain.

**ABOVE:** Roses were replanted by the National Federation of Gardening after a thorough investigation of what roses were popular in the 17th century.

**OVERLEAF:** A spectacular view of the patio with its four parterres framed in boxwood hedge.

# THE FRANZ MAYER MUSEUM

Franz Mayer, the German financier who was in love with Mexico until his death in 1975, bequeathed Mexico the collection housed in this museum, which was the ancient San Juan de Dios Hospital, constructed as a two-story building in the second half of the sixteenth century. It holds one of the most important decorative-arts collections in Mexico.

The patio was designed "so that God could see it," and from the upper part, through the arcade, we can see a quadrangular space with four entrances. At the center there is a seventeenth-century fountain decorated with an eight-pointed star, drawn with yellow, green, and white tiles from Puebla.

The parterres around the fountain have a trapezoidal shape; they are surrounded by tiny laurel leaf shrubs *(Laurus nobilis)*, boxwood trees *(Buxus sempervirens)*, and a few benches here and there. As we go down the narrow outside staircase, we can see three ash trees and a privet in the opposite corners. Pots with azaleas *(Azalea hybrida)* are placed between the arcade's columns.

**OPPOSITE:** The admirable square patio was built in the second part of the 17th century.

**ABOVE:** Azaleas in pots between limestone columns that frame the patio.

**ABOVE RIGHT:** The central fountain is decorated with green, yellow, and white tiles from Puebla and forms an eight-pointed star that evokes a mariner's compass. A composed hedge of boxwood and gold Japanese spindle tree grows.

**OPPOSITE:** In the foreground, a candelabra aloe (*Aloe arborescens*).

**TOP:** A view of the park where peacocks and pre-Hispanic dogs walk freely through the lawns among eucalyptus, green ebony, coral trees, pepper trees, and privets.

**ABOVE:** An Aztec head next to a potted cactus.

**ABOVE RIGHT:** The pots once contained grains, spices, sugar, honey.

## DOLORES OLMEDO MUSEUM

In the area of Xochimilco, not far from the *chinampas,* or floating gardens, there is a majestic hacienda known as La Noria, which dates back to the sixteenth and seventeenth centuries.

Dolores Olmedo, who has owned the property since 1962, was responsible for its reconstruction. Here old pepper trees, eucalyptus, coral tree, green ebony, and pokeweed, a tree of pre-Hispanic origin with an immense trunk, provide shade.

The "Orange Tree Patio" got its name from the seven fruit trees that grow here. During the colonial period, large red pots were filled with grain, spices, sugar, and honey. Today, lying on the volcanic-stone ground, they hold calla lilies, geraniums, bougainvillea, roses, and hydrangeas. Throughout the year the plants paint the patio in different colors: deep red with the poinsettias in winter, lilac green ebony in spring, and white calla lilies in the interim.

La Noria, with all its attractions, merits a visit. It is a mix of pre-Hispanic pieces in a colonial garden with the art collection of Frida Kahlo and Diego Rivera, two of the most significant figures in twentieth-century Mexican painting.

# EL JARDÍN BORDA

**OPPOSITE:** A view of one of the main allées bordered by butterfly palm and an Australian umbrella tree. This is the only original colonial garden still existing.

**ABOVE:** Detail of the white fountain with columns in the corners.

**ABOVE RIGHT:** Large pond where one of the most lavish parties of the colonial times was celebrated. Emperor Maximilian and his wife, Empress Carlota, selected this place to be their summer residence.

In 1865, after a trip to Yucatán, the emperor Maximilian and his wife, the empress Carlota, chose this site in Cuernavaca as their summer residence. Maximilian, whose interest in botany was well known, enjoyed his stay here, often holding formal meetings with the members of his court in the gardens and concerts on the stage next to the pond. Intricate legends of grand love affairs were woven here.

In the years to come important guests visited the Jardín Borda, such as Francisco I. Madero, Emiliano Zapata, Porfirio Díaz, and Diego Rivera.

Among the plants and flowers that can be seen in the garden are philodendron, azaleas, golden-trumpets (*Allamanda cathartica*), guavas, syngonium (*Syngonium* sp.), Jacob's-coat (*Acalypha wilkesiana*), bougainvillea, fishtail palms (*Caryota mitis*), brown areca palms, *muñequitas*, angel's-trumpet (*Brugmansia arborea*), tabachín (*Delonix regia*), dumb cane (*Dieffenbachia amoena*), loquats, rose apple (*Eugenia jambos*), *flor de Pascua (Euphorbia pulcherrima)*, Indian laurel (*Ficus retusa*), windowleaf (*Monstera deliciosa*), ferns (*Nephrolepis exaltata*), rose-bay (*Nerium oleander*), avocado trees (*Persea americana*), yuccas (*Yucca elephantipes*), tamarind (*Tamarindus indica*), and African tulips (*Spathodea campanulata*).

## ROBERT BRADY FOUNDATION

Robert Brady, an American, left an enchanting legacy: a restored sixteenth-century house in Cuernavaca, also known as Casa de la Torre (Tower House); at the time it was the Episcopal Palace.

The main patio re-creates in detail the intimacy of Franciscan monastic gardens. The most interesting thing in this patio is its vertical design: on one side we have the nineteenth-century tower from which the house takes its name, and on the other, the sixteenth-century cathedral with supporting walls covered with vines.

Fifteen different types of wild orchids may be seen against the wall that supports a fountain made of glazed tile from Puebla, along the double staircase leading to the tower. A magnificent huamuchil (*Pithecellobium dulce*), a hundred or two hundred years old, is located in the patio, as a living sculpture.

The modern-art collection, with paintings by Frida Kahlo and Milton Avery, among others, is eclectic and personal. There are pre-Hispanic pieces in the garden and arts and crafts in every corner.

**OPPOSITE:** The fountain is set against the green wall covered with creeping fig (*Ficus pumila*) and orchids.

**TOP:** Creeping fig frames a carved stone image of the Virgin of Guadalupe.

**ABOVE:** The verticality of the patio can be appreciated with its 19th-century tower covered with windowleaf.

**ABOVE RIGHT:** The patio re-creates the intimacy of the Franciscan gardens.

## THE DIPP GARDEN

**OPPOSITE:** The 17th-century arcade is surrounded by elephant´s-ear plants *(Alocasia macrorrhiza)* and is shaded by ashes.

**ABOVE:** As in Young Plinio's gardens, trees are covered with canary ivy *(Hedera canariensis)* around an old well.

**ABOVE RIGHT:** An old ash covered with canary ivy and windowleaf plant frames the 17th-century arcade that is now part of the garden.

**OVERLEAF:** A colorful area of the tropical garden *(top left)*. A pebbled allée is surrounded by ash trees, rubber trees, and windowleaf plants *(bottom left)*. Another part of the garden is planted with banana trees *(right)*.

The San Jorge ranch is an extended property of over ten acres situated on the west side of Guadalajara. For decades it has been surrounded by a dense urbanistic development, so the ranch and its gardens are a green island in the middle of an urban city.

For over half a century, the Dipp family has worked to turn it into a sophisticated, lush, rich, and varied residential garden. What was once horseland was developed by the family following the rules of the best fruit and vegetable gardens in Jalisco, with mostly local species.

Historical architectural elements were recovered from the demolition of large stately homes and set on the grounds. The large nineteenth-century arcade came from the military hospital; today, as a loggia, it gives the garden a personality of its own. Another arcade dating back to 1612 has been placed in a corner of the garden.

## MOORISH INFLUENCE

A formal garden in Monterrey, influenced by the Moorish gardens of southern Spain, was created by its owner purely by willpower, given the arid nature of the region.

This garden contains two kinds of elements: the vertical and the horizontal. The vertical ones, which can be appreciated in two rows of cypress trees, high plants, walls, and tall hedges, prevent the monotony that tends to characterize large, grassy areas. The combination of both elements creates some striking moments in the garden. Of particular note is the interplay of the cypress and the central fountain, built in the Italian style.

The views from the house or from various points in the garden provide us with the horizontal elements: irises and fragrant plants lining the brick paths, a fountain, and the sets of red roses surrounded by boxwood trees *(Buxus sempervirens)*.

**OPPOSITE:** The tall cypresses contrast with the trimmed parterres of roses and boxwood tree hedge. At the end of the allée: flax lily.

**ABOVE:** Water lilies float around the Italian fountain set against the Sierra Madre at sundown.

**ABOVE RIGHT:** Climbing ivies on a pergola frame a line of cypresses.

**OVERLEAF:** The Italian-style fountain is bordered by daisies and, farther away, by roses.

## CHAPTER IV

Hacienda Gardens

The word *hacienda* takes us to a dream world where we romanticize our childhood memories, the times we played at our grandparents' house in those large patios or gardens and everything tasted sweet, like *ate*, the dessert made from guava. What is this strength in the magic of the haciendas that has stayed with us and still permeates our reality?

The story of the haciendas begins with the conquest of Mexico. The celebrated Marquise de Calderón de la Barca described life in the haciendas during the mid–nineteenth century, when they were mostly developed "as splendid and solid constructions with big gates opening to the main patio. From there, one could see the outer buildings, the stables, and the *trojes* [granaries] as well as flourishing orchards that I visited when I traveled from one hacienda to another."

She would tell how she walked out into the orchard. "We never went in without a long stick as there would be furious guardian geese at the entrance." And she added: "In the late afternoon . . . we went to the orange orchard where three thousand blooming trees formed avenues that could be literally seen drooping their branches loaded with the golden fruit and their snowlike blooms. I had never seen such a beautiful view. Each tree is perfect and as tall as any other tree in the forest. The ground was covered, under its broad shades, with thousands of oranges that had ripened and fallen, as well as white and smelly flowers."

The nineteenth-century bourgeoisie transformed the old patios and the uncultivated land in the main-house area into beautiful gardens that they and their visitors would enjoy.

Water fountains refreshed the gardens' atmosphere. A series of trees was planted to produce shade on benches and kiosk corners, paths or greens. Strollers would stop by to talk here while they enjoyed the greenery and shrubs around them. Beautiful bronze or marble statues adorned the place, and competed with the cages filled with multicolored birds that enriched the delightful views and sounds.

There are haciendas everywhere in Mexico: sugarcane-growing ones in Puebla, those that produce tequila in Jalisco, the cattle haciendas in the north, and so forth. We have selected two lesser-known areas: the coffee-producing haciendas in Veracruz and the hemp haciendas in Yucatán.

The once prominent hemp haciendas are now being rescued and restored. Various buildings like Temozón, Santa Rosa de Lima, San José Cholul, and Katanchel have been transformed into luxurious country houses or hotels, leaving behind their once-important productive function.

**PAGE 90:** The allée that leads to this ex-hacienda chapel is bordered by golden summer daylily, lollipops (*Pachystachys lutea*), and tree ferns.

**PAGES 92–93:** An imposing *pich* (in Maya) or elephant's-ear (*Enterolobium cyclocarpum*) in the main entrance of the Santa Rosa de Lima Hacienda, redesigned and run as a hotel by Plan Arquitectos, in Yucatán. Under its branches grow philodendron, malanga (*Xanthosoma robustum*), Moses-in-the-cradle (*Rhoeo discolor*), and wildflowers.

**OPPOSITE:** A view of the Valderrama garden near Coatepec, Veracruz. In this humid climate, virgin's palm and pigmy date palm grow well.

**ABOVE:** Pansy orchids (*Miltonia x hyeana*) grow in the Valderrama garden.

## EL LENCERO

The former Hacienda El Lencero is now open as a museum. The history of the hacienda began in 1525, when it was part of the eleven inns located on the road from Veracruz to Tenochtitlán (which would later become Mexico City). In the nineteenth century, it belonged to the famous General de Santa Anna, who was president of Mexico eleven times, losing Texas and later selling California to the United States. At the time, the property had approximately 4,336 acres.

The tranquil hacienda has been well restored and decorated, and its pond is embroidered with parterres of yellow lilies (Hemerocallis flava).

As you arrive, you must walk along a path of Indian laurel trees. They say the benjamin fig (Ficus benjamina) in one of the gardens is three hundred years old; it offers a splendid view as it is surrounded with a carpet of balsam and philodendron. After the Tule tree in Oaxaca, this benjamin fig is one of the most important trees in the country.

**OPPOSITE:** The spectacular fig in front of the hacienda.

**ABOVE:** A view from the back garden with kaffir lily (Clivia miniata) in the front and a duck pond on the right.

**ABOVE RIGHT:** A sea of golden summer daylily; the fig with the farm in the back.

**OVERLEAF:** A wrought-iron gate with a bronze symbol of the Aztecs—the eagle devouring a snake—opens onto the field of golden summer daylily, the magnificent fig, and the hacienda.

## HACIENDA KATANCHEL

In Katanchel, the new pioneers Aníbal and Mónica González have recovered the glory of the past to grant it to a select group of learned bird watchers, archaeologists, botanists, and lovers of nature. Their challenge has been to re-create the natural, pre-Hispanic precolonial habitat. (The place had been abandoned for thirty years.) Aníbal González, the architect, has restored the hacienda, and his wife Mónica Hernández, the botanist, preserves and cares for the species of plants that had been known by the Mayas.

Just like any hacienda in Yucatán, it was built following a perfect geometry in perspective and along a perfect axis: multicolored painted stucco walls, rounded stairs, classical iron gates, ponds, and fountains. All these elements give life to the grass squares, the rows of trees planted long ago: silk-cotton trees *(Ceiba pentandra)*, the sacred trees of the Mayas, who thought their boughs would take them to heaven and their roots to hell; palm trees; fig trees; and other fruit trees.

During the rainy season, there are butterflies and fireflies, so many it seems someone were breeding them. Mónica Hernández has managed to re-create the three levels of jungle vegetation and preserve it.

**OPPOSITE:** The principal bungalow of the hacienda has a verandah covered with blue trumpet vine.

**TOP:** The mysterious pistachio *(Pistacia vera)* garden is shaded most of the time. With its fountain in the center it has a classical and romantic design.

**ABOVE:** A detail of a Yucatecan garden. The "green gold," or century, plant, used to manufacture sisal ropes, among other things, was most important before nylon was invented.

**ABOVE RIGHT:** The magnificent arrival at Katanchel hacienda. A *pich* on the right is covered with pothos *(Epipremnum aureum)*.

PAGES 102–3: Bougainvilleas and papaya *(Carica papaya)* cover the façade of the pavilion.

1. Elephant's-ear and lobster-claw plants grow in this luscious garden.

2. A wall made of Mayan stones is surrounded by malanga, windowleaf, and nephthytis *(Syngonium podophyllum)*.

3. Papyrus grows inside a Mayan carved stone.

4. An amate, or fig, grows and covers the wall with its roots.

5. A path of calcarian sand goes through the rich flora of the Katanchel gardens.

OPPOSITE: Lobster-claws.

## SACCHICH HACIENDA

Built one hundred years ago by Italian architects—who also built the famous Peon Contreras theater in Mérida—the Sacchich hacienda belonged to the same family until Mrs. Rosa Maria Barrera López bought it twenty years ago. It had been a hemp-producing property. Today it is an important nursery, supplying many gardens of Yucatán and sending plants and flowers all over the world.

Gardeners have been trained there and Mrs. Barrera López feels it is giving work to a large community. They cultivate mainly varieties of palms such as bottle palm *(Hyophorbe lagenicaulis)* and fishtail palm *(Caryota mitis)*; fruit trees such as litchi *(Litchi chinensis)*, naseberry *(Manilkara zapota)*, star apple *(Chrysophyllum cainito)*, mammee *(Mammea americana)*, and tamarind *(Tamarindus indica)*; and trees from the region such as teak *(Tectona grandis)*, siricote *(Cordia dodecandra)*, and touch-me-not *(Mimosa pudica)*.

**OPPOSITE:** The surprising Islamic arch, typical of the 19th-century architecture of the haciendas in Yucatán, is the entrance to Hacienda Santa Rosa de Lima, managed by Plan Arquitectos.

**ABOVE:** In Hacienda San Antonio Sacchich, Acanceh, bougainvilleas of different varieties and colors grow together.

**ABOVE RIGHT:** The neoclassical hacienda has been turned into an important nursery that serves all of Yucatán. On the left, the tall column is in fact the trunk of a royal palm *(Roystonia regia)*.

## SAN JOSÉ CHOLUL

Situated in the heart of the ancient Maya province of Cehpech, in Yucatán, San José Cholul, Plan Arquitectos, has preserved important aspects of architecture from the early nineteenth century, when the hacienda focused on raising cattle and growing corn. *Henequen,* or sisal fiber, had not yet become the main product of the hacienda; this happened at the end of the nineteenth century.

Conveniently located between the towns of Tixkokob, Euan, and Kakalchen, San José Cholul is one of only a few isolated *henequen* plantations that never formed a village of its own. Today it is a small Plan Arquitectos hotel full of charm and history and the flavor of once-upon-a-time. At a short distance, major Mayan archaeological sites and colonial monuments such as the Motul convent can be visited.

**OPPOSITE:** Century plant and Moses-in-the-cradle grow in front of the early-19th-century façade of the old *hacienda henequenera.* Restored by Plan Arquitectos.

**ABOVE:** Shaving-brush tree *(Pseudobombax ellipticum),* which blooms in early spring.

**ABOVE RIGHT:** In the old hacienda, leadwort *(Plumbago capensis)* and bougainvilleas grow together.

**ABOVE:** The garden of San José Cholul, with wandering jew *(Zebrina pendula)*.

**RIGHT:** Purple-heart at the entrance to San José Cholul.

**OPPOSITE:** The garden of Hacienda Yokdzonot, with a colonial fountain in the center, parterres, and potted Indian laurels in each corner.

**OVERLEAF:** Horses are a major presence in Yokdzonot, where they freely gallop through the fields. Rows of *Ficus benjamina* fig grow on parterres of orange jasmine *(Murraya paniculata)*. In the center is a colonial fountain.

## CHAPTER V

Gardens of Luis Barragán

Poetry and mystery, serenity and bewitchment—these are the pillars on which the Barragán gardens stand and bloom.

When the great architect and landscape designer received the Pritzker Award, Barragán remarked in his acceptance speech: "You have to make homes become gardens and the gardens, home. Intimacy and home should be there, in the enclosed gardens. You can't trust a garden that is open-wide and reveals everything at first sight."

Barragán's entire work revolves around gardens. He was strongly drawn to them—so much so that everything he created, with his talent and magnificent sense of style, was directed toward the living experience of gardens, which were basically rooms of the houses he designed.

You can't talk about his gardens and avoid mentioning the great influence that the French writer Ferdinand Bac, the Alhambra, and Mediterranean culture had on Barragán. He learned that a panoramic view should not be captured but should be framed.

Mystery really does take hold of those who are fortunate enough to enter Barragán's world. But one has to be prepared to proceed gradually—only then can one grasp the gardens' essence, their underlying virtue. Barragán enclosed his gardens behind walls covered with climbing plants. He planted tall trees with shorter ones in front to mask their trunks and lawns to cover the ground all around. He did not like grounds that had to be raked or trees that had to be pruned. He taught us how to grant plants their freedom instead of cutting them down. For Barragán every living, growing thing was a sculpture—that was how he loved them and enjoyed them. Architect Andrés Casillas remembers his teacher's advice on how to plant trees: take a handful of marbles and cast them out as far as you can; where every little bead falls, there plant a tree.

Barragán is one of the few Mexican architects to have gone beyond the private garden into the public space of the big city. He planted avenues with eucalyptus in Las Arboledas. There, the fountains of tall colored walls hold the space of running water that refreshes the environment. He makes us feel the sex appeal of gardens and all their ambiguous elements, their mystery and poetry in what used to be hard and wild landscapes. "In the gardens and homes I've designed, I have always endeavored to allow for the placid murmur of silence. In my fountains, silence sings."

## PRIETO LÓPEZ GARDEN

Luis Barragán's landscaping is centered in El Pedregal de San Angel, a volcanic area in the southern part of Mexico City, which was formed when the Xitle volcano erupted 2,500 years ago. In recent years, the urban gardens have been almost totally destroyed or abandoned because the city has grown toward the west. Barragán turned this area into one of the most important urban developments in Mexico City.

In 1945, Barragán sold to his friend Eduardo Prieto López and his wife, Esther, a piece of volcanic land with crests and circles of petrified lava, like the waves that spread concentrically from a stone cast in the water. Here he literally framed the view of the distant volcanoes, the Popocatepetl, the Iztaccihuatl, and the Ajusco: these were the real "pictures" that "hung" in the house. The view changes when seen from each different cardinal point.

The garden is monochrome green with old trees, like pepper trees and ash trees. The true Mexican colors are on the walls: the Prieto López garden is no exception.

**OPPOSITE:** The wall of the house has been painted the color of the coral tree *(Erythrina americana)* in autumn, indigenous to Mexico.

**ABOVE:** A volcanic-stone staircase leads from one part of the garden to the other.

**ABOVE RIGHT:** A detail of fruit and seeds of the coral tree.

**ABOVE:** A view from the upper garden. Gardens, patios, and porches are one more room of Barragán's inner home. A tortuous coral tree, elms, and jasmine find their way around a green lawn, important to most of Barragán's gardens.

**RIGHT:** Barragán played with water and silence in the gardens. The colonial fountain reflects serenity and bewitchment.

**OPPOSITE:** A spectacular lava formation is covered with fallen bougainvillea flowers.

**OVERLEAF:** A detail of 19th-century limestone sculptures representing souls in hell *(left)*. They are surrounded by candelabra aloe. The climate permits it: the Prieto López lunch outdoors all year long under an ash covered with ivy *(right)*.

## GALVEZ GARDEN

The site for Casa Galvez was chosen by Barragán because of the beauty of the eucalyptus, ash, and fig trees that bloomed majestically there, and around which he built this important house in 1955.

In the entrance patio, a fig tree blooms behind a low yellow wall that serves as a bench and hides its trunk. A beautiful narrow fountain murmurs between tall, shocking pink walls and a window, two of Barragán's trademarks.

In the main garden, on the other side of the house, a screen of yellow jasmine shrubs hides a green field that leads to a red brick patio and a theater, a most unusual site.

"It is important to stress," said Barragán, "that gardens, especially in certain climates and regions of the world, be a year-round living room, where you can sit, eat, and get together with others." And that is what the Galvez family does in this perfect space.

**OPPOSITE:** A view from the red patio, with a spineless yucca *(Yucca elephantipes)*, eucalyptus, and bougainvillea.

**TOP:** A detail of the red patio with a fig tree *(Ficus carica)* and ivy.

**ABOVE:** The discovery of the Mexican-pink wall from the perspective of the red patio.

**ABOVE RIGHT:** The red brick patio where children come and play.

**ABOVE:** The patio outside the servants' quarters, planted with Abyssinian banana trees *(Ensete ventricosum).*

**RIGHT:** Barragán built this house around the ash and eucalyptus trees that were there. He accepted the job for the beauty of the trees.

**OPPOSITE:** Volcanic-stone tiles and grass lead to a screen of jasmine and to the red patio. Note the clean change of level in the lawn, a typical Barragán signature.

## CHAPTER VI

Contemporary Gardens

Due to the modernist movement's notion that green space was unnecessary, the garden gradually lost its glamour. It became a historical site, a living monument to be seen from afar.

But now, people are turning once again to the garden. Modern man, when seeking his roots, evades everyday life in order to show his power and cultivate his individuality, his differences. When we recover our sense of place, our consciousness, we realize that gardening could be the path to recoup our humanity. Gardening allows us to give concrete form to an idea, an ideal, a haven where we may observe things in detail.

Technology surrounds us and we ask ourselves over and over again: What seems to be more real today? The garden where we take a stroll, take a deep breath of the various scents, and let ourselves feel, or the world we visit on the Internet or see on television? We are recovering our awareness and discovering that the garden is not dead, but rather, alive, as a privileged form of our imagination.

In Mexico, one is able to take delight in gardens all year round, because of the climate. In cities like Guadalajara, Monterrey, or Mexico City, contemporary gardens tend to be green; flowers are few; they follow a rigorous design in which the trees stand out.

When we visit a garden, we would do well to choose those details we particularly like, the ones we'd like to remember, and set aside those elements that seem superfluous. We should concentrate and think about what pleases us. Then, we might be driven to ask: How would that look in my own garden?

The gardens that I like most have been planned and designed; they focus more on visual effect than on botanical collection, with many different species that, on their own, may be remarkable. But there is no single concept of the contemporary Mexican garden. It varies according to each creator, each landscape. Some clearly have a colonial stamp, others are beholden to Luis Barragán, while many have captured the minimalism of Oriental serenity. Finally, some resemble piñatas, with their explosion of color and exuberant forms.

**PAGE 130:** Simplicity of design in a patio in Monterrey by landscape architect Adán Lozano.

**PAGES 132–33:** A small, lush garden by landscape architect Ernest Arnolt for architect Carlos Herrera's office in Mexico City, as seen from a corridor.

**OPPOSITE:** Fernando Solana's patio in Mexico City was designed by architect Teodoro González de León and the landscape architect is Robin Velarde. Ivy covers the beams as well as the tall walls that isolate the patio from the big city.

**ABOVE:** The very personal patio of José de Yturbe. Rows of agaves on brightly colored steps give this patio, located in the heart of Mexico City, the feeling of being in a Jalisco hacienda or in a country house.

## CASA PALACIOS

**OPPOSITE:** The mysterious and rustic path between the Prieto and Palacios gardens, which were one large Barragán garden before the marriage of Jana Prieto to Roberto Palacios.

**ABOVE:** Fire thorn (*Pyracantha coccinea*).

**ABOVE RIGHT:** A shaded path with candelabra aloe, ivy, philodendron, and windowleaf.

**OVERLEAF:** Ivy, rather than grass, covers the soil (*top left*). Pots sit casually on the patio (*bottom left*), as in any Barragán garden. Notice how nature takes over the architecture, ruling the patio (*right*). ·

Contemporary architects who follow Luis Barragán opt for color. Natural pigments from this land, so rich and strong, cover the walls.

José de Yturbe designed this house in the garden where Jana Prieto de Palacios was raised. The patio is square, uncovered, and immense. The floor is made of volcanic stone with pots full of philodendron. The purple bougainvillea contrasts with the mammee color of the walls and the climbing ivy. Here, Jana recalls, was the cave where she used to hide and play at age three.

"We like it in winter and summer, during the day and at night. We feel sheltered by the large walls," say the owners.

As one goes beyond the patio and reaches the volcanic-rock garden, covered with trailing vegetation, three wooden troughs create something resembling a family—the direct inspiration of The Lovers, the Barragán fountain in Las Arboledas.

## ELECTRA GUTIÉRREZ'S GARDEN

When Electra and Tonatiuh Gutiérrez were looking for a house in the 1980s, they knew they wanted one with a garden that would penetrate the house. The garden came first. What they found is located in the heart of colonial Coyoacán, a block away from the zócalo. Their friend, architect Ricardo Legorreta, planned with them an inner garden filled with ferns—an homage to Le Douanier Rousseau—and remodeled the house with large windows and openings that bring the garden inside.

The green ebony trees were there and, for a couple of months a year, shed their flowers on the grass, forming a purple rug that delighted the Gutiérrezes. "It is like a rain of purple flowers," they had said.

Electra and her late husband enjoyed the selvatic jungly look. They had breakfast among the flowers, surrounded by squirrels begging for a few crumbs, savoring it all every day.

OPPOSITE: A romantic corner of the Gutiérrez's garden.

TOP: A wooden wheel from Oaxaca seems like a piece of sculpture in the garden; it serves as a table.

ABOVE: A tree fern grows under a privet tree.

ABOVE RIGHT: The green ebony trees are dropping flowers on the lawn. On the left, the wedding flower (*Dombeya wallichii*) also blooms.

# THE GUZMÁN HOUSE

Architect Francisco Guzmán and his wife, Maricarmen, chose to live in this house in Mexico City, built on approximately 5,000 square meters of land (eventually divided into four houses with gardens by Guzmán Giraud & Bernardi Arquitectos). Blocks of architecture were conceived using natural materials from the region so the contemporary Mexican look would be enhanced. And the garden is integrated into the house.

The staircases were done in treated pine wood, as was the deck, with intertwined vines along each step leading to the main entrance, planted with a row of orange trees. "The garden was planted for adults," comments Guzmán. "We did not want a football field, as most people with small children request. This garden is a space of encounter with oneself."

Papyrus *(Cyperus papyrus)* in the entrance, dietes *(Dietes vegeta),* a weeping willow *(Salix babylonica),* and tropical parterres complement the south garden.

**OPPOSITE:** Papyrus sits in a reflecting pool; lemon trees border the *tepetate* (volcanic rock) wall.

**TOP:** The orange trees are planted in pebbled jardinières as a border inlaid in the wooden floor.

**ABOVE:** With risers covered with ivy, the staircase becomes a part of the garden.

**ABOVE RIGHT:** French lavender is used as ground cover.

**OVERLEAF:** On the wooden floor, a bottle ponytail *(Beaucarnea gracilis)* from La Huasteca region. Behind it grow bird-of-paradise *(Strelitzia reginae),* tree ferns, and mondo-grass *(Ophiopogon jaburan).*

OPPOSITE: The garden has a large variety of plants, pruned in different shapes.

TOP: The garden as seen through the pool with a potted Mexican fan palm in the foreground.

ABOVE: African lily (Agapanthus africanus), angel wing (Begonia sp.), heavenly bamboo (Nandina domestica), and lollipops.

ABOVE RIGHT: The volumes of these trimmed shrubs are architectural.

OVERLEAF: Two aspects of the same garden, where bushes take the shapes of stones: the rustic in the foreground, the manicured in the background.

# A GARDEN IN LOS SABINOS

Achieving good color in the garden is similar to achieving a good design in a house. It means training the eye. Undoubtedly the owners of this garden in Monterrey have done so; they were selective and exercised extremely good judgment.

Color comes from the generous use of mock-orange, variegated mock-orange, wheeler's dwarf, and Chinese silver privets from Puerto Rico, trimmed in the shapes of balls and mushrooms, which do well in the heat and the cold. Balsam with a touch of silver leaves from the sycamore poplars, heavenly bamboo, boxwood trees, junipers, African lilies, daylilies in lime yellow, and rocks located in specific parts of the composition create the impression that you're going down a mountain.

The variety of geometric and abstract shapes is almost unlimited. It's as if the garden had been specifically created to fit the house. Nothing, not one single herb, is out of place, no ivy vine is longer than another, nor are there any withering flowers. This garden is outlined, combed, shaped, watered, and fed with extreme care and detail. The soft presence of flowing water allows this perfection to flourish.

## THE VALDÉS HOUSE

Built in 1985 against the skyline of the spectacular Sierra Madre, this large yellow contemporary house was in fact designed in Luis Barragán's office. Barragán was too ill to travel, so Raúl Ferrera, a partner, developed the project. Consuelo Valdés would also come to Mexico and spend time with Barragán. She remembers discussing the colors with him.

The house is built around six patios but Valdés enjoys the main patio best, playing there with her grandchildren and swimming daily in the pool. Because the mountains are so strongly present, and the house so vivid in its color and dimension, the patios are planted with lawns that bring peace to the whole concept with the added color of a few boungainvilleas.

**OPPOSITE:** The shaded entrance to the house has jardinières of bougainvillea against the yellow wall.

**ABOVE:** A detail of the main patio with coral trees on the right and the peaceful green lawn on the left.

**ABOVE RIGHT:** The back patio with bougainvillea growing on the wall.

**OVERLEAF:** The patio is framed both by the Sierra Madre and coral trees.

## CHAPTER VII

The Garden and Personality

In his book *The History and Art of Gardening* John Dixon Hunt writes: "Gardens express or incarnate specific people, cultures, periods, and places. Men and women create environments for themselves or for a particular society or culture. Through them they expand the dimensions of the real world."

Both natural and artificial, the garden always has something of the two; it is a miniaturized image of its surroundings, representing and revealing them.

Painters, sculptors, writers, film stars—all create a particular atmosphere that the garden reflects and magnifies. The garden functions as a frame, a laboratory for its owner's fantastic imagination.

In the land they develop and find the creativity that makes them so original. That is, the artist's garden, that which belongs to someone famous, holds the seed of that which makes them famous and different. This cosmos is not superficial. Something must inspire and transmit the owner's sensitivity.

Modern gardens are essentially personal. Let us take a look at them, big and small, in the city or in the countryside: it is that sense of personal choice and determination that makes them interesting. The great designer and landscape architect David Hicks was most selective; he wanted to see what each garden entailed: an art gallery, a museum, or a historical site.

**PAGE 154:** Actress María Felix's garden in Cuernavaca, the eternal-spring city.

**PAGES 156–57:** In sculptor Juan Soriano's patio, his 1991 *Sirena,* or mermaid (bronze, 98 X 30 X 47 cm.), among malanga *(Xanthosoma robustum).*

**OPPOSITE:** A view of the main patio in Frida Kalho and Diego Rivera's Blue House. Magnolias and green ebony in bloom add color to the very personal and unusual patio.

**ABOVE:** A magnolia—a flower often painted by Kalho—in full bloom.

## OCTAVIO PAZ FOUNDATION

In this house, in this garden, Nobel laureate Octavio Paz lived his last months with his wife, the artist Marie-José Paz. She continues to look after the foundation that was created for her husband in 1997.

La Casa de Alvarado, in Coyoacán, is Spanish colonial dating back to the eighteenth century, and one of the most outstanding houses in the Santa Catarina barrio.

The main door, the skylights, the patio, and the terraces have that "sun made time," as Octavio Paz used to describe some constructions in the Valley of Mexico. The poet's words resonate among these walls, dissolving in this garden of light: "Mexico is a solar country . . . a country rich with sun, extravagant with sun, it is also a black country, a dark country."

In the past, the main path used to cut across a circular greenhouse. This has since disappeared, but the garden preserves the sweet enchantment of semiabandonment without having lost its original design.

Two jardinières with trimmed benjamin figs and ferns mark the entrance to the garden. The potted plants that decorate the first patio seem to mirror the sun and clouds.

**OPPOSITE:** The main colonial patio with fishpole bamboo *(Phyllostachys aurea),* ferns, and benjamin fig.

**TOP:** This is the garden where Paz spent the last months of his life with his wife, the artist Marie-José Paz. It is filled with old pines and ash trees.

**ABOVE:** A corridor bordered by walls of ivy and azaleas. Tall ash trees stand in the back.

**ABOVE RIGHT:** An Aztec serpent head adds drama to the garden.

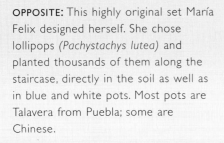

## MARÍA FELIX'S GARDEN

**OPPOSITE:** This highly original set María Felix designed herself. She chose lollipops *(Pachystachys lutea)* and planted thousands of them along the staircase, directly in the soil as well as in blue and white pots. Most pots are Talavera from Puebla; some are Chinese.

**ABOVE:** The pool is bordered with potted plants. Italian sculptures and busts animate this façade of the house. The pool reflects turtles, María's favorite animals.

**ABOVE RIGHT:** A detail of lollipops.

**OVERLEAF:** A brick and blue tile built-in bench framed by Talavera pots filled with lollipops.

At the beginning of the new millennium María Felix is perhaps the only living myth of Mexican film. She has been a muse to great composers such as Agustín Lara and José Alfredo Jiménez. We remember her in movies like *Maclovia* (1948), *Doña Diabla* (1950), *Enamorada* (1946), *Doña Bárbara, La Cucaracha* (1958), *Tizoc* (1957), and *La Valentina* (1965).

"The garden is a perpetual feast," María says. "In my garden I always feel extremely happy. I never feel sad there."

The ravines that Malcolm Lowry describes in *Under the Volcano* are typical of Cuernavaca. María Felix has made good use of them, creating a terraced garden that flows downhill toward a dry riverbed that fills with water in the rainy season. Viewed from below, the hillside looks like a tropical jungle.

Thirty-three steps lead from the swimming pool to the pavilion at the bottom of the ravine. There is a fountain at each level, with melodious water running through little canals. The seductive effect of plants, flowers, tiles, and urns reveals the personal touch of a great Mexican actress.

Chinese-porcelain urns decorate the terraces, each of which features a single kind of flower. This is the essence of María's style: less is more.

**1.** A bronze faun sculpture on a tile base is surrounded by lollipops.

**2.** The enchanting mirrored pavilion where María Felix loves to dine under the Charles X chandelier. The table and *azulejos* on the bench are Portuguese.

**3.** More lollipops. Too much is just enough.

**OPPOSITE:** A view of the garden toward the pavilion, or *merendero,* and the barranca. In the background, two Norfolk Island pines *(Araucaria heterophylla).*

## GABRIEL AND ANTONIETA FIGUEROA'S GARDEN

**OPPOSITE:** The shaded garden with rows of potted balsams at the foot of an ash and a border of fleur-de-lis *(Iris x germanica)*. The bench was part of a Mexican public park in the 19th century.

**ABOVE:** Climbing senecio *(Senecio* sp.*)* in bloom.

**ABOVE RIGHT:** The path from the house is bordered by hortensias *(Hydrangea macrophylla)*.

Gabriel Figueroa, the great cameraman and photographer, and his wife, Antonieta, lived in Coyoacán, a quaint neighborhood known for its architecture and narrow cobblestone streets. The colonial door that takes you into the home provides a grand sensation of peace and harmony.

A wide central path leads to a small garden, the "star garden," the most important place in the house. It's designed in such a way that one can see it from any part of the house. Pear, walnut, orange, lemon, plum, and pomegranate trees seem to whisper the secrets woven in the forty years that Antonieta and Gabriel lived together until his death.

The immense retaining wall, colored deep blue, blends in with the blue sky; here one feels a touch of the sublime. "I have oranges and lemons, pears, figs, plums, pomegranates, and walnuts; the squirrels come and take them," Antonieta laughs. She is so full of life and she thanks the garden for that. For their son, Gabriel Figueroa Flores, a filmmaker and photographer like his father, that garden was his universe. "I had no brothers, only sisters. The garden was my playmate, a laboratory to observe nature, to see how the little animals behaved and how the plants grew."

# EDWARD JAMES'S GARDEN

Edward James designed a surrealist garden in the Huasteca Potosina, near Xilitla, about forty-three miles from Ciudad Valles. With no formal training in architecture, James made his architectural dream come true in this dense, isolated jungle. In the process he gave Mexico one of its most fantastic gardens.

The natural son of Edward VII, Edward James is a friend and patron of surrealist painters like Dalí and Magritte, as well as neo-Romantics like Pavel Tchelitchew.

This is an enormous garden of some seventy-four acres. A moss-covered brush fence encloses the space. Structures of painted concrete and iron are well integrated into this exuberant natural area that engulfs Greek temples, pagodas, and Gothic and Romantic palaces. Time is suspended here.

We are in a garden that seems to have sprung from Arabian poetry. It is a monument to surrealism in Mexico, with an upside-down Mayan arch leading to a room with a single bench that wiggles like one of the serpents on a pre-Hispanic temple, in front of a fireplace begging for a blaze.

**OPPOSITE:** In the middle of the humid Huasteca Potosina jungle, the magic garden of Edward James.

**ABOVE:** A snake of concrete is reminiscent of the Aztecs.

**ABOVE RIGHT:** A Gothic pavilion reminds us of Edward James's Scottish roots.

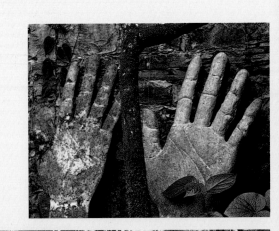

Different aspects of this surrealist
garden where sculpture and nature
interact in a most unusual way.
Structures of painted concrete and
iron are well integrated into this
exuberant natural world—a boundless
world of mystery and moss.

## CHAPTER VIII

Gardens Near Mexico City

Mexico City and New York City have something in common. They're so intense, so exhausting, that their residents want desperately to get away on weekends to be in touch with nature, recuperate in peace and harmony, achieve well-being and a balanced family life. The green presence of nature embraces us, soothes us, and makes us feel better.

The beauty of the landscape in this region was undoubtedly one of the main reasons why the Aztecs put an end to their mythical pilgrimage in the Valley of Mexico, founding one of the most magnificent cities of the time and developing a sophisticated cult of gardens.

This same beauty and diversity of landscape has been the source of inspiration for the garden culture that has emerged in Mexico's central region—one that has grown extensively due to the wondrous conditions of climate, water quality, and the large number of vegetal species in the region.

The unbeatable climate in Tepoztlán, Cuernavaca (the "city of eternal spring"), and Valle de Bravo is but one reason why many *chilangos* (as Mexico City residents are known) have country homes in these places. In the gardens there they can express all their creativity. The splendid vegetation flourishes and may be enjoyed year-round.

The extraordinary quality of the water (due in part to the aquifers from the volcanic mountainous area to the north) contributes to making the entire valley of Cuauhnahuac a garden paradise. In this garden, nature's time is revealed—that which lives and dies, from a stone to a tree. Mexico's central region provides invaluable sources of inspiration and elements of landscape for the creation of beautiful gardens that fit perfectly into their surroundings.

Landscape architects such as Eliseo Arredondo, Ignacio Colín, and Juan Guzzy have chosen to work in this valley. As Ignacio Colín says, "The garden is ultimately a fragment of nature that has been reproduced by the hand of man, the landscape is his source of inspiration, and its cultivation is the thread that links us to our essence."

**PAGE 174:** The González Carbonell garden in Tepoztlán with a Sebastian sculpture in the middle of the lake and the view of the Tepoztecan mountains behind.

**PAGES 176–77:** The Yolanda Quezada garden in Cuernavaca. Quiet and serene, with areca, royal palms, green ebony, and azaleas in bloom.

**OPPOSITE:** Pink quills *(Tillandsia cyanea)* bloom on a green ebony in a patio in Tepoztlán.

**ABOVE:** The Josefina Quezada garden in bloom with two pink poul trees *(Tabebuia rosea)* shading the pool.

## THE AUTHOR'S GARDEN

My land used to be a corn plantation, encircled by pine trees with two rather lonely jacarandas. Farther beyond, the spectacular rocky mountain known as Tepozteco—also the name of an Aztec pyramid located at the mountain's top—is reminiscent of certain kinds of landscape found in Tibet.

I wanted to frame the spectacular view but did not want to reveal all its secrets at once. There are orange and lemon trees, avocados, bananas, and a loquat tree, as well as bamboo to form interior boundaries and screens of luxuriant papyrus. There's a bit of color here and there for contrast, and an edge of violets and nasturtium, but even then, the garden is almost totally green.

My friend, the architect Luis Barragán, had a great deal of influence on this garden. In 1982, when work started, he was already ill and unable to come to see it. But from his home in Tacubaya we agreed on a grassy area on the foreground that would automatically lead us to see the mountain in all its magnificence. Barragán insisted on the importance of having a tranquil space that would contrast with the "Wagner-like" quality of the mountains. He made one concession: a small orchard.

**OPPOSITE:** A small adobe bungalow is covered with poet's jasmine, camellia, and a yellow Chinese hibiscus.

**TOP:** Lobster-claw in bloom.

**ABOVE:** In front of a wall of papyrus: butterfly lily, a lovely fragrant white ginger, and a Mexican bush sage.

**ABOVE RIGHT:** Under the green ebony tree grows the guardian of the garden: an unusually large pulque agave.

**OVERLEAF:** A fishpole-bamboo wall encloses the pool area, with bird-of-paradise, Indian-shot, common garden canna, nasturtiums, false globe-amaranth, and Mexican bush sage.

**OPPOSITE:** There are more than 300 species in this garden: among them, staghorn fern *(Platycerium bifurcatum).*

**TOP:** Detail of a tailflower *(Anthurium andraeanum).*

**ABOVE:** A shaded and jungly-looking corner of the garden, ideal for a siesta.

**ABOVE RIGHT:** Lemon and orange trees and azaleas grow around the spot where Charlot and Drumbolis have tea.

**OVERLEAF:** The colonial fountain as seen from the house. Bird-of-paradise *(Strelitzia reginae)* on the left.

# THE CHARLOT AND DRUMBOLIS GARDEN

The garden of American actress Juli-Lynne Charlot and landscape architect Ken Drumbolis contains numerous plant species; some of them are from Mexico, the rest Ken himself has brought from all over the world.

Drumbolis has created a journey of initiation to nature. The wide path made of soil slowly leads toward the house covered with jasmine vines. This is the most luxuriant part, with jacarandas on each side of the path, high yuccas and avocado trees with native flowers creating a woodsy and mysterious atmosphere that contrasts sharply with that of the street and lets the visitor get carried away to a secret world.

Different varieties of tailflowers *(Anthurium andraeanum),* native to southeastern Mexico, various wandering jews *(Zebrina pendula),* and long-lasting spiderworts *(Tradescantia* sp.), easy to cultivate in Tepoztlán's strong, changeable climate, complete the landscape at the entrance. Several small paths lead to the colonial fountain, to the round table where Ken and Juli-Lynne drink tea and watch the sunset.

"In terms of the landscape, it's a garden, although an enclosed one, with certain vistas that carry us to other subliminal spaces, other atmospheres," Drumbolis says.

**OPPOSITE:** The lake, with the red Sebastian sculpture, is bordered with patient lucy *(Impatiens wallerana).*

**TOP:** A wall of cypresses marks the start of the cactus field.

**ABOVE:** Rocks in the reflecting pool form paths.

**ABOVE RIGHT:** Terraces of tree ferns and patient lucy.

**OVERLEAF:** Spectacular sculptural garden among the terraces and pools of the house, with the Tepoztecan mountains in the back.

## PABLO AND GABY GONZÁLEZ CARBONELL'S GARDEN

When he was a child, businessman Pablo González Carbonell became familiar with Tepoztlán, and it is with love and great devotion that he worked over each and every inch of one of the most spectacular gardens in the state of Morelos. He worked with architect Eduardo Terrazas, who built the house around the garden; they decided to raise the level of the construction site in order to be able to enjoy the whole view of Tepozteco, the imposing mountain, without having to trim the trees.

Water is ever present. It is found in the fountain's murmur, in the mirror that encircles the house and creates its reflection, in the pool, and, farther down, in the lake, where several sculptures by Sebastian stand next to a spectacular Indian tulip.

This space has three divisions: the manicured garden, the orchard, and the nurseries, where they keep one of the most varied collections of cacti in Latin America.

The most important element in this garden is Tepozteco; without its overpowering presence in the background, the garden would not have the magical quality it does.

# JONACATEPEC GARDEN

The Jonacatepec garden is undoubtedly one of the most beautiful, varied, and well-cared-for gardens that can be found in a semitropical climate in Mexico. It is located only a few blocks from the central square in Jonacatepec, a small, picturesque town in the state of Morelos.

The garden, built around forty years ago, has been conscientiously cultivated and cared for by Luis Felipe del Valle Prieto. It has an important and varied collection of exotic plants such as *Cactaceae*, orchids, palms, succulents, and many other tropical and semitropical species. Fruit trees grow in abundance: guava, avocado, macadamias, sapodilla, and mammee.

"Many of the rare plants I've found come from tiny villages, where people planted them, lovingly, in the most incredible large pots you can imagine," says del Valle.

The garden's efficient design, the way it is laid out, its variety, and the care he's put into it make it a paradise where one can truly appreciate nature at its best.

To date, the Jonacatepec garden contains more than 1,300 species. Many of them are on sale to the public in the nursery, which recently opened. The proceeds go to the garden's upkeep.

**OPPOSITE:** An allée of queen palms *(Arecastrum romanzoffianum)* towers over croton *(Codiaeum variegatum)* and Australian fountain palm *(Livistona australis)*.

**TOP:** Royal palm in bloom.

**ABOVE:** Detail of a sausage tree *(Kigelia pinnata)*.

**ABOVE RIGHT:** An extremely well kept and important garden with more than 1,300 species.

## SAN GABRIEL IXTLA, VALLE DE BRAVO

In the mid-1990s Tullia and Ricardo Salas, two gifted designers, fell in love with a ranch dating back to the eighteenth century. Their main target was to plant the garden first. They found and planted cherimola trees *(Annona cherimola)*, as well as criollo avocados and wild plum trees. They restored an important cactus field of prickly pears. The main hill around the house is covered with pulque agave and wild lavender. In the naturally rocky and arid zone of the garden, local century plants have been replanted.

And so the Salases' objective is being achieved: a natural garden that respects the lunar and solar cycles and bows to the rainy season from June to September, a natural garden where rabbits, foxes, armadillos, and many birds are returning.

**OPPOSITE:** An orchid grows on a cherimola tree.

**ABOVE:** Wild lavendar grows between the leaves of an agave.

**ABOVE RIGHT:** A corner of the wild garden, with century plants, pipe organ cactus, barrel cactus, and serpent cactus.

**OVERLEAF:** Surrounded by a conifer forest, a hill of century plants, prickly pear, and wildflowers next to the Salas ranch, which dates back to 1790.

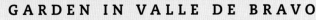

## GARDEN IN VALLE DE BRAVO

Here we see one of the most spectacular views of Valle de Bravo, that of the lake and its mountains. The house was built twelve years ago by the great architect José de Yturbe, a follower of Luis Barragán. In order to preserve the environment and the beauty of the rocks nearby, the house and its terraces were built with a rocklike substance of poured concrete. The house seems to be naturally sitting on an extension from La Peña, the rock that gives its name to the area.

The different cacti, indigenous to Mexico, have been collected by the owners themselves along their hiking paths (both are ardent sportsmen). Among the cacti are century plants (*Agave attenuata*), barrel cactus (*Ferocactus latispinus*), and hen-and-chickens (*Echeveria gibbiflora*). Others, typical of the region, form a natural fence along the ravine below.

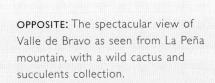

**OPPOSITE:** The spectacular view of Valle de Bravo as seen from La Peña mountain, with a wild cactus and succulents collection.

**ABOVE:** The entrance of a typical Valle de Bravo house next to La Peña.

**ABOVE RIGHT:** The view from the tiled and pebbled terrace.

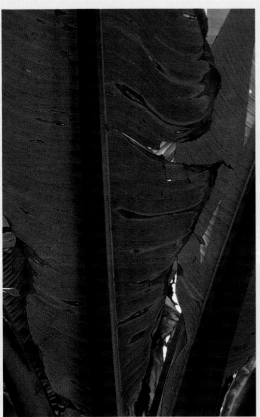

## THE HAGERMAN GARDEN

OPPOSITE: An important part of the garden consists of potted plants along the many corridors and terraces of the house.

ABOVE: Abyssinian banana leaves (*Ensete ventricosum*).

ABOVE RIGHT: This corridor leads to the entrance of the house. On the wall hangs a collection of stonecrop (*Sedum* spp.).

OVERLEAF: Pots and more pots link one area of the garden to the other (*left*). In the foreground rests a pre-Columbian frog, one of the most important protectors or guardians of the gardens in ancient mythology. Orchids are planted in a hanging pot (*right*).

"Our garden has not been planned," say Eduardo and Graciela Hagerman. "It grows according to how we feel. The garden very much resembles our own life, and by the same token, it holds the memory of our childhood." In a certain way, Hagerman pictured the books of childhood in the garden. He built several bridges over the barranca, which transforms itself into a torrent during the rainy season. And with it, aromas and colors are enhanced in this junglelike garden where nothing is trimmed—nothing but the plants in their collection of four hundred pots with which the Hagermans play and like to change from patio to patio. Among them are numerous orchids, camellias (*Camellia japonica*), bird-of-paradise (*Strelitzia reginae*), succulents, and azaleas (*Rhododendron indicum*), as well as medicinal plants. Everything grows in this tropical climate.

## CHAPTER IX

# Gardens Along the Coasts

Mexico has just under 5,400 miles of coastline, but even in the 1960s there was little notion of a seaside garden; the sea was the garden of the houses.

In 1970, with architect Marco Aldaco, Loel and Gloria Guinness built the first modern house with a *palapa*. They planted aromatic and exotic plants to create what to this day is one of the most important gardens on the Pacific coast. And in other places along the coast an awareness of gardens began to evolve: in Cancún, Huatulco, Ixtapa, Los Cabos. The generous climate makes this possible.

In Los Cabos, Baja California, desert gardens can now be found. The rose glow of sunset is sharper here, an elongated cloud hugs the horizon, the sky turns pure turquoise. Now, too, in Baja, Japanese and American styles with Mexican plants achieve a new type of garden. Nature is only slightly changed here, and very little maintenance is needed. This combination of natural forms and hills planted with palm trees slopes down to the sea. The setting reminds us that this is not a garden set apart, the way that a European garden would be, but part of the larger garden embodied in the Sonoran Desert, where it rains only occasionally.

The floodgates are now open. Gardeners and landscape architects alike respond to the landscapes and climate of the Pacific, the Caribbean, the Gulf, creating with nature and shaping it. These are the gardens of the new century, truly Latin and worlds unto themselves. As Luis Barragán and Ferdinand Bac have said, "a well-designed garden contains nothing less than the entire universe."

**PAGE 204:** A view of the bay of Careyes from Las Casitas, planted with potted bougainvilleas and coconut palms.

**PAGES 206–7:** A large border of blue agave, from which tequila is extracted, and a torote tree (*Bursera* sp.) are part of the spectacular desert garden at Las Ventanas al Paraíso Hotel.

**OPPOSITE:** The Pössenbacher geometric patio at Casa Caimán, with its central fountain, desert fan palm, and the typical pots from Jalisco, with colorful bougainvilleas.

**ABOVE:** A view from Mi Ojo, the first house in Careyes designed by Marco Aldaco. The garden is planted with coconut and areca palms.

## LAS VENTANAS AL PARAÍSO HOTEL

In this part of Baja California, the mountains from the Sierra de San Rafael and the Sierra de la Giganta meet. There are streams that come down from the mountains toward both coasts—on one side the Pacific, on the other the Sea of Cortés. They are the protagonists in this grand scene. Often they are dry, but underneath the surface, crystalline water flows, providing for the regional vegetation. The desert, which is usually viewed as an empty space, is fertile soil for an infinite variety of *Cactaceae*, and in this spot landscape designer David Thompson from SWA group has created an oasis. Most of the plants come from different parts of the Baja peninsula; the torotes were rescued from a garbage heap. At Las Ventanas al Paraíso people are extremely concerned about preserving the environment and the local flora. All the plants, with the desert sands and the streams with their slow, uneven currents, help us remember that *las ventanas al paraíso* means "the windows of paradise."

**OPPOSITE:** Desert plants native to the Baja California peninsula form this garden. Here, pipe organ cactus and barrel cactus.

**ABOVE:** One of the many hummingbirds that fly and suck honey from the flowers.

**ABOVE RIGHT:** Like a set, the entrance of Las Ventanas al Paraíso is a combed sand field planted with blue agaves and date palms.

1

2

3

212 Paraíso Mexicano

4

6

5

1. A hummingbird approaches a flowering agave.

2. An agave planted against the wall, made of royal palm, of a hut.

3. Prickly pear cacti (*Opuntia* sp.) from Arizona and northern Baja California.

4. A pulque agave is about to bloom, the one and only bloom of its life.

5. A sotol plant (*Dasylirion acrotriche*).

6. An ocotillo (*Fouquieria splendens*), without leaves during the dry season.

**OVERLEAF:** Pink prickly pear, with golden spines *(left)*. Young candelabra aloe *(Aloe arborescens)*, sotol plant *(Dasylirion acrotriche)*, and torote trees *(Bursera* sp.) *(right)*.

## CASA DEL ORIENTE

For the garden at Casa del Oriente, the colors garden designer Sofía Brignone chose were lilacs, purples, yellows, oranges, and white.

The *papelillo rojo* (*Bursera* sp.), whose thin and transparent red cortex appears to go up in flames at sunset, and the *pata de cabra (Bauhinia variegata),* or orchid tree, are two trees we find in Casa del Oriente. Most significant, though, are the *terracerías* (a Mexican terraced landscape) inspired by Japan's Zen gardens.

The *terracerías* blend in totally with the house. But it has been necessary to "domesticate" them through the geometric trimming of the plants and the placement of fine stones and combed sand (as in Las Ventanas al Paraíso), to create the effect of fish bones. It is, says Sofía Brignone, "a Mexican interpretation of Zen."

**OPPOSITE TOP:** A view of the ocean from Casa del Oriente.

**OPPOSITE BOTTOM:** Two geometrical structural jardinières planted with fountain grass (*Pennisetum* sp.) and bougainvilleas.

**ABOVE:** Two Japanese-inspired *terracerías* frame a pipe organ cactus in bloom.

**ABOVE RIGHT:** Flowers of yellow sage (*Lantana camara*) at the foot of a coconut palm.

## PUNTA IXTAPA

The entrance to Punta Ixtapa is marked by a *barota*—symbol of the respect Mario Lazo and Diego Villaseñor, both architects, hold for the exuberance of nature. The impression it gives is that they decided it was better left untouched. This is one of the most spectacular and well-built residential resorts by the Pacific.

Working with teams of biologists, physicists, and botanists, the architects chose not to use any exotic plants. As a result, the gardens are mostly green, with few flowers—except for the guaiacum (*Guaiacum sanctum*), which blooms in spring, the orchids from Yucatán—creating an impressive sensuousness that carries us elsewhere, to a different vegetation of various characteristics and sizes, with other hues in the leaves, and other flora. Nothing has been contaminated here; nature has remained unchanged.

**OPPOSITE:** In Troncones, Christmas palm, Chinese hibiscus, and bougainvilleas grow.

**TOP:** Coconuts grow freely along the Pacific coast.

**ABOVE:** The allées are shaded from the sun by bamboo roof structures, which create a pleasant pattern on the walkways.

**ABOVE RIGHT:** A lush and green pathway to one of the apartment buildings.

## CASA LOS PALMARES

The idea of Los Palmares sprang from an old friendship between the owners of the property and Marco Aldaco, the architect and landscape architect who would rather be known as the advocate of "integrated architecture."

We could refer to the gardening here as "spontaneous," one that takes advantage of the irregularities in the terrain. Aldaco planted strong, lasting leaves in the foreground—ocean grapes to protect the more delicate plants, like jasmine and ferns. In the patios, sheltered from the strong ocean breeze, he planted more ferns and Hawaiian palms, fan palms, and star palms, which are fragile when facing the wind but do well in the shade; and orchids, which need shade and humidity.

The "integrating" architect was forced to design a landscape of *Cactaceae* over the ocean due to what the landscape offered and the steep inclination of the land. This formed a natural hill of magnificent cacti and prickly pears that do not trap the rainwater and thereby take root easily. The waves break against the cacti and create a dramatic effect.

**OPPOSITE TOP:** A view from the garden toward Las Cuatas beach, with a mirador from which to see the sun set.

**OPPOSITE BOTTOM:** The staircases to the main house are framed by jungle geranium *(Ixora javanica),* purple-heart *(Setcreasea pallida),* and bougainvilleas.

**ABOVE:** A sea of purple-heart resists sea winds and brings color all year long.

**ABOVE RIGHT:** Jungle geranium, purple-heart, and bougainvilleas against the retaining wall.

## XPU-HÁ

Gardens on the Caribbean coast differ from those in Baja California or along the Pacific. The region is most often planted with flowers and exotic bushes that are not native to the area, but they resist the hurricanes that tend to hit the coast every so often.

There is one exception: at Xpu-Há ("morning dew" in Mayan), Carlos Moreno's garden stands, magnificent on the white Caribbean sands. It is situated one hour from Cancún, next to pre-Hispanic ruins and sixteenth-century convents. The hammocks made in Yucatán hang from the trunks of *chit* palms, or thatch palms *(Thrinax radiata)*. Immense white coral from this beach now lies in repose on the grass, encircled by a gray-green "ash" ivy, on both sides of the narrow path leading to the beach. The coral reef protects this space from the incoming ocean winds, isolating the garden and retaining the sand during the cyclone season. The garden is small; it was left to grow with no particular plan while the house was being built, at the swaying rhythm of the Mayan hammocks and the turquoise-colored waves.

**OPPOSITE:** The garden as seen from the first floor of the house, with coconut palms and the shrub *Tournefortia gnaphalodes.*

**ABOVE:** Detail of a fan palm leaf.

**ABOVE RIGHT:** Pioneer shrub *(Tournefortia gnaphalodes)* protects the sand and the garden from hurricanes and strong winds.

1

2

3

1. Young coconut palms.

**2 and 3.** Coral stones found on the beach punctuate the St. Augustine grass *(Stenotaphrum secundatum)* around southern swamp leaves *(Crinum americanum)*.

**OPPOSITE:** The romantic view of the beach penetrating the garden.

**OVERLEAF:** A Mayan hammock, perfect for a nap in this glorious Caribbean atmosphere. Coconut palms grow tall and strong in the St. Agustine grass *(Stenotaphrum secundatum)* and the shrub *(Tournefortia gnaphalodes)* in front of the beach.

Gardens to Visit

## DOLORES OLMEDO MUSEUM

5843 Av. México, La Noria, Xochimilco, Mexico DF

Location: Near the La Noria local train, heading toward Xochimilco

The majestic sixteenth-century estate called La Noria is located near the famous floating gardens of Xochimilco. The buildings cover 6,000 of the estate's 32,000 square meters.

Mrs. Dolores Olmedo bought the property in 1962 and rebuilt the southern and western ends of the original structure, along with what was left of the roof supports. She later acquired adjoining land and planted gardens with pepper trees (*Schinus molle*), eucalyptus (*Eucalyptus* spp.), coral trees (*Erythrina americana*), jacarandas (*Jacaranda mimosifolia*), lilies (*Crinum x powellii*), and calla lilies (*Zantedeschia aethiopica*). Peacocks and *xoloizcuintles* (small dogs from pre-Hispanic times) rove the grounds.

The museum has the largest and most important collection of Diego Rivera paintings in the world, as well as works by Angelina Beloff—Rivera's first wife—and Frida Kahlo. There are also works of pre-Hispanic art and Mexican folk art.

It is one of the city's most important museums, not to be missed.

Best time to visit: Year-round
Phone: (52) 56 76 10 55/55 55 12 12
Fax: (52) 55 55 16 42
Hours: 10–6 Tuesday–Sunday
E-mail: manager@mdop.org.mx

## XOCHIMILCO ECOLOGICAL PARK

1 Periférico Oriente, Col. Ciénega Grande, Xochimilco DF 16070

Location: On the Periférico Oriente between Canal de Cuemanco and Av. Canal de Chalco, in front of the plant, flower, and garden produce market

This is one of the most successful projects of the Ecological Rescue Plan (PEX), designed to rehabilitate the Xochimilco area when it was declared a UNESCO Patrimony of Mankind in 1987. It is part of a complex that also includes a flower and vegetable market and a sports stadium. Conceived as an educational as well as a recreational facility, PEX has an information center and an arboretum of plants native to the central Mexican plain. Designed by the well-known landscape architect Mario Schjetnan, it sponsors more than four hundred events a year.

In Nahuatl, Xochimilco means "the place where they plant flowers." Although it is all that remains of the system of lakes destroyed in the wake of the Spanish conquest, it continues to be the principal source of water for the largest city in the world.

One of the Rescue Plan's principal goals is to protect the world-famous *chinampas*, or floating gardens, that are the very symbol of Xochimilco.

A *chinampa* is an artificial island made out of the lake's own mud and roots, which are held together by the remarkable native trees called *ahuejotes* (*Salix bondplantiana*).

With 215 hectares (of which 50 are water), Xochimilco is one of the most extensive green areas in the city. It can be visited on foot, by bicycle, pedal boat, tourist train, or *trajinera*—one of the characteristic vessels of the *chinampa* lakes and canals.

Don't miss the chance to ride a *trajinera*, go for a picnic, or simply stroll through this park to the sound of mariachis.

Best time to visit: Year-round
Peak times: Saturdays and Sundays
Phone: (52) 56 73 78 90
Fax: (52) 56 73 76 53/80 61
Hours: Summer: 9–4 daily
Winter: 10–4 daily
E-mail: garciaa@servidor.unam.mx

## UNIVERSITY OF MEXICO BIOLOGY INSTITUTE BOTANICAL GARDEN

Circuito Exterior (unnumbered), Ciudad Universitaria

Location: The UNAM-IB Botanical Garden includes the Faustino Miranda greenhouse, on the Ciudad Universitaria campus, and the Outer Botanical Garden, on the Circuito Exterior

The garden is situated in the Pedregal de San Angel, a rock formation created when the Xitle volcanic chain erupted approximately 2,500 years ago. It is in the southwestern part of the Valley of Mexico, at 2,320 meters above sea level.

The Botanical Garden's collection specializes in agaves and cacti. It sponsors scientific investigation, educational activities, conservation, and recreation. Each of its areas is divided according to the taxonomy and geographical range of the plants and their ecological and cultural importance.

Here tourists from abroad can appreciate the great plant diversity of Mexico. Climates represented range from the arid to the temperate and the warm-and-humid; there is also a section of plants known for their usefulness. The 110-hectare Pedregal de San Angel Ecological Reserve is adjacent to the Botanical Garden. Its virgin scrub forest is the only one of its kind in the world.

Best time to visit: Year-round. The garden organizes guided tours, courses, conferences, concerts, and workshops. The Tigridia gift shop sells items decorated with unusual botanical motifs.
Phone: (52) 56 22 90 47/63
Hours: 9–4 daily, except holidays and university vacations
E-mail: www.ibiologia.unam.mx

### FRIDA KAHLO HOUSE AND MUSEUM
247 Londres, Col. del Carmen, Coyoacán, México DF 04100

Location: The house, which was built by Kahlo's parents in 1904, is five blocks from the Coyoacán central square, near the market.

The most famous woman painter in Latin America lived here with her husband, the muralist Diego Rivera, until her death in July 1954. Together they made a point of decorating the house in a purely Mexican style.

The garden reflects the personalities of its famous owners. In it Diego built an Aztec-looking pyramid to house his collection of pre-Hispanic art.

With a magnificent southern magnolia (*Magnolia grandiflora*) in its center, the garden has fine specimens of lilies (*Crinum × powellii*), wax-leaf privet (*Ligustrum lucidum*), jacarandas (*Jacaranda mimosifolia*), cacti, and calla lilies (*Zantedeschia aethiopica*), Diego's favorite flower.

Best time to visit: Year-round
Phone: (52) 55 54 59 99
Hours: 10–6 Tuesday–Sunday

### LUIS BARRAGÁN HOUSE AND MUSEUM
14 General Francisco Ramírez, Col. Amplición Daniel Garza, Mexico DF 11840

Location: Between Constituyentes Avenue and Gobernador José Ceballos, behind the Constituyentes subway station

Luis Barragán's garden in Tacubaya was designed as part of the house, which he built in 1947. Recently restored to its original design, it is a required visit for garden lovers.

Barragán believed that gardens should be "poetical, mysterious, suggestive, and gay." Of his garden designs he remarked, "Silence sings in the fountains." This garden embraces an entire universe of sensual and emotional experience.

Architect Louis Kahn commented about it: "[Barragán's] garden is surrounded by a high wall: the land and vegetation remain as he found them, untouched. . . . Although only a tiny stream of water flows through his gardens they are so huge that all the landscape designs in the world together can't touch them."

In the words of the Nobel Prize–winning novelist José Saramago: "This garden is a world in itself, as if the entire world were contained in it, as if there were no other world."

Best time to visit: Year-round
Phone: (52) 55 15 49 08/52 72 49 45
Hours: By appointment 10–2 and 4–6 Monday–Friday, 10–1 Saturday
E-mail: cmlbmex@df1.telmex.net.mx

### CASA DE LA BOLA MUSEUM
136 Parque Lira, Col. Tacubaya, Mexico DF 11860

Location: Next to Lira Park

The Casa de la Bola began as an olive plantation. Considerably modernized in the nineteenth century, it was established as a museum by Don Antonio Haghenbeck y de la Lama and is now a registered historical landmark. Its lovely romantic garden has many elements from the colonial period, including benches, ponds, pools, and clay conduits.

Among the plants and trees currently represented are wax-leaf privet (*Ligustrum lucidum*), jacarandas (*Jacaranda mimosifolia*), tepozanes (*Buddleia cordata*), evergreen ashes (*Fraxinus uhdei*), blood-trees, eucalyptus (*Eucalyptus* spp.), cypresses (*Cupressus* spp.), yuccas (*Yucca* spp.), Abyssinian bananas (*Ensete ventricosum*), tree ferns (*Cyathea* spp.), and windowleaf (*Monstera deliciosa*). Flowering plants include acacias (*Acacia* sp.), magnolias (*Magnolia grandiflora*), camellias (*Camellia japonica*), eugenias (*Eugenia* sp.), calla lilies (*Zantedeschia aethiopica*), cannas (*Canna × generalis*), heliconias (*Heliconia uxpanapensis*), giant honeysuckle (*Lonicera hildebrandiana*), fuchsias (*Fuchsia* sp.), and irises. Among the fruit trees are black sapotes (*Diospyros digyna*), cherimolas (*Annona cherimola*), Japanese medlars (*Eriobotrya japonica*), and mulberries (*Morus* sp.).

The house has a broad selection of decorative arts from the sixteenth to the nineteenth centuries. A walk through its rooms gives a good sense of nineteenth-century Mexican life.

Best time to visit: Year-round
Phone: (52) 55 15 55 82
Hours: Guided tours by appointment 9–5 Monday through Friday, 11–5 Sunday

### CHAPULTEPEC CASTLE GARDEN
Location: In the Chapultepec hills within the forest's First Section, corner of Reforma and Gandhi. Chapultepec subway station

In Nahuatl, *Chapultepec* means "locust hill." The castle, which houses the National History Museum, is located at the top of this outcropping, the highest point in the Valley of Mexico. The original structure dates from the eighteenth century.

The gardens and arbors to the west of the complex were designed in the 1920s by architect Antonio Rivas Mercado, at the request of President Alvaro Obregón. From this spot there are magnificent panoramic views of the city.

The stone stairways with pre-Hispanic serpents' heads on the north end of the garden were added during the building's conversion to a museum.

The fountain is an Art Deco oval with motifs inspired by plant life, like pineapples and grapes.

The museum features four centuries of Mexican history. It offers guided tours, a library and archive, bookstore, cafeteria, and recreational and educational activities.

Best time to visit: Year-round
Phone: (52) 55 53 62 24/55 55 62 02
Fax: (52) 55 53 62 68
Hours: 9–5 Tuesday–Sunday

## SENIOR CITIZENS PARK

Location: Corner of Molino del Rey Street and Reforma in the First Section of the Chapultepec Forest, Miguel Hidalgo District

The garden of the Euquerio Guerrero Senior Citizens Park was created by people over sixty years of age, representing the full range of socioeconomic and educational backgrounds. It sponsors sporting and recreational events as well as courses, lectures, guided tours, walking tours, and Sunday dances.

More than 20,000 square meters in area, the garden has a large collection of modern sculpture and 300 species of orchids in a lovely building managed by the Mexican Orchid Growers Association.

The greenhouse includes "lion's-paw" philodendron (*Philodendron selloum*), Amazon lilies (*Eucharis grandiflora*), "leather-leaf" spathe flower (*Spathiphyllum* spp.), slipper shrubs (*Pedilanthus* sp.), "goat's-face" tree ferns (*Alsophila* sp.), anthuriums (*Anthurium* spp.), painted nettle (*Coleus blumei*), papayas (*Carica papaya*), calla lilies (*Zantedeschia aethiopica*), "cat's-claw" mimosa (*Mimosa* sp.), Mexican breadfruit (*Monstera deliciosa*), hollyhock begonias (*Begonia gracilis*), calatheas (*Calathea* sp.), mafafas (*Xanthosoma robustum*), rabbit's-foot ferns (*Phlebodium aureum*), "foxtail" lupines (*Lupinus elegans*), malquique tree ferns (*Cyathea* sp.), frangipani (*Plumeria rubra*), bamboo palms (*Chamaedorea seifrizii* and *Rhapis excelsa*), papyrus (*Cyperus papyrus*), and fishtail palms (*Caryota mitis*).

Best time to visit: Year-round
Phone: (52) 52 56 26 33
Fax: (52) 52 71 06 09
Hours: 9–2:30 Tuesday–Sunday

## FRANZ MAYER MUSEUM

45 Av. Hidalgo, Col. Centro,
Mexico DF 06300

Location: In front of the Central Alameda, Bellas Artes subway station

The museum is housed in the former Hospital of San Juan de Dios, a two-story structure from the second half of the sixteenth century. The seventeenth-century fountain in the center of the square courtyard is decorated with yellow, green, and white tiles in the shape of an eight-pointed star.

The courtyard is divided into smaller areas by low hedges of bay laurel (*Laurus nobilis*) and boxwood (*Buxus sempervirens*).

In opposing corners, there are azaleas (*Azalea hybrida*) and camellias (*Camellia japonica*).

There are benches in the garden where one can sit and listen to the birds.

Franz Mayer was a German financier who lived in Mexico and upon his death left provisions for the creation of the museum.

Best time to visit: Year-round
Phone: (52) 55 18 22 65
Hours: 9–5 Tuesday–Sunday
E-mail: fmayerc@data.net.mx

## FORMER CONVENT OF THE DESERT OF LIONS

Location: The ruins of the convent are 18 miles west of Mexico City, on the highway to Toluca, Edo de México

Founded in 1604, the convent was originally named Holy Desert of Our Lady of the Carmen of the Mountains of the Holy Faith. It is situated at 2,790 meters above sea level in the middle of 21 square kilometers of hills, ravines, waterfalls, and streams. The recently opened Hermitage Walk (Paseo de las Ermitas) connects nine hermitages in the surrounding area.

Pines (*Pinus* spp.) predominate in the cool mountain climate, although one also finds "oyamele" firs (*Abies religiosa*), oaks (*Quercus* spp.), arbutuses (*Arbutus* sp.), black cherries (*Prunus serotina* 'Capulli'), and sour cherries (*Prunus cerasus*). There are treasure flowers (*Gazania rigens*), pansies (*Viola tricolor*), hortensias (*Hydrangea macrophylla*), and roses (*Rosa* sp.). The wildlife includes bluebirds, woodpeckers, quails, red-tailed hawks, coyotes, white-tailed deer, raccoons, squirrels, rabbits, *teporingos* (a kind of rabbit), *tlacuaches* (opossums), and rattlesnakes.

Despite the rich plant and animal life that surrounds this ancient place, the lingering spirit of contemplation gives it a special charm. One has the option of visiting either the convent grounds or the woods: the peace, simplicity, and quiet of the convent are in sharp contrast with the city.

There are splendid views of the ancient buildings as well as the colonial gardens, which were redesigned in the 1970s by architect Eliseo Arredondo. There is a good restaurant, convenient bus service, and picnic grounds.

Best time to visit: Year-round
Phone: No phone
Hours: 6–5; the former convent opens at 10 Tuesday–Sunday

## COSMOVITRAL: THE STAINED-GLASS WINDOW GARDEN OF TOLUCA

Location: In Toluca, less than 40 minutes by car, west of Mexico City

This botanical garden is situated within an Art Nouveau mansion on the Plaza de España. The former city market, it was built in 1910 to celebrate the centenary of Mexican Independence. In 1978 artist Leopoldo Flores installed a series of stained-glass windows representing his vision of time, movement, and the universal dialectic of matter. Because the windows tell the story of mankind's journey through a cosmic cycle, they are intimately related to what goes on around the building.

The botanical garden covers 5,000 square meters, of which 3,500 are dedicated to 400 plant species from various parts of Mexico, Central and South America, Africa, and Asia.

The garden contains mostly exotic plants in re-creations of their natural environments. Among them are giant ferns (*Cyathea americana*), palms (*Chamaedorea* spp.), dracaenas, lilacs, aroids, gingers, aralias (*Aralia* sp.), aphelandras (*Aphelandra* spp.), philodendrons (*Philodendron sagittifolium*), and succulents.

There are in addition a Japanese garden and various fountains and ponds.

Best time to visit: Year-round
Phone: (52) 72 14 67 85
Hours: 9–6 Tuesday–Sunday
E-mail: gemseimc@mail.edomex.gob.mx

## TEZOZOMOC PARK

Manuel Salazar y Zempoaltecas, Col. Prados del Rosario, Mexico DF 02410

Location: Behind the Azcapotzalco CCH

A scale model of the Valley of Mexico in the sixteenth century, Tezozomoc Park reproduces the original five lakes and topography. It was designed by landscape architect Mario Schjetnan in consultation with historian Tomás Calvillo. The obelisks symbolize the geographical location of the valley's original features.

The architect was asked to create a living museum that would speak to us about its past and invite us to muse on who we are and why we are here.

Landfill from subway construction was used to contour the land, and the recycled water is from a nearby treatment plant. Most of the plants are native to the Valley of Mexico, although others have been introduced over time. Belonging to the first category are the mescals (*Agave parryi*), pepper trees (*Schinus molle*), Xochimilco ahuejotes (*Salix humboldtiana*), willows (*Salix* sp.), evergreen ashes (*Fraxinus uhdei*), coral trees (*Erythrina americana*), irises (*Iris x germanica*), "foxtail" lupines (*Lupinus elegans*), pampas grass (*Cortaderia selloana*), papyrus (*Cyperus papyrus*), and Oldham bamboos (*Bambusa oldhamii*).

Best time to visit: Year-round
Phone: (52) 53 82 72 09
Hours: 6–6 Tuesday–Sunday

## XOCHITLA FOUNDATION

Tepotzotlán, Edo de México 54600

Location: 45 minutes north of Mexico City in Tepotzotlán, near the magnificent colonial building that houses the National Museum of the Viceroyship

In Nahuatl, *xochitla* means "place with many flowers." The Foundation is accordingly intended to be a permanent green space in which people can reconnect with nature so as better to enjoy and understand her. It has gardens, forests, and substantial areas that have been left in their natural state.

With 70 hectares, Xochitla is one of the few areas in the northern Valley of Mexico set aside as a green space. The Foundation is a nonprofit institution dedicated to working with society to develop and protect the natural reserve. In addition to the grounds, Xochitla has impressive views and a pleasant restaurant, as well as a school for gardeners.

Best time to visit: Summer and fall
Phone: (52) 58 95 03 86/92 and 94
Hours: 9–6 daily
E-mail: contacto@xochitla.org.mx

## BORDA GARDEN

271 Av. Morelos, Col. Centro, Cuernavaca, Morelos 62000

Location: Near the Cuernavaca Cathedral

There are only two gardens in Mexico that survive from the colonial period: the Borda Garden and the Pensil Mexicano Garden in Mexico City. The Marquis of Borda, a wealthy miner from Taxco, bequeathed the house and lands to his son, Manuel, a priest who changed the property into a planting garden.

Part of his contribution is the Guadalupe Church, which is thought to have one of the most beautiful domes of any Mexican church.

A giant pond (or small artificial lake) was built for the most celebrated fêtes of colonial times.

In 1865 Emperor Maximilian and his wife, Carlota, chose the site for their summer home. Because of his interest in botany Maximilian was especially drawn to the gardens.

The Borda Garden is a must for those who go to Cuernavaca. Its gardens have been visited by Francisco I. Madero, Emiliano Zapata, Sebastián Lerdo de Tejada, Francisco Leyva, Porfirio Díaz, Diego Rivera, and numerous other celebrities. It is currently the home of the Morelos Institute of Culture, which sponsors art shows and festivals of dance, theater, and music.

Best time to visit: Year-round
Phone: (52) 73 18 10 38/14 02 82
Hours: 10–5:30 Tuesday–Sunday
E-mail: scultura@morelos.edomorelos.gob.mx
Web site: www.morelos.edomorelos.gob.mx

## ROBERT BRADY FOUNDATION

4 Netzahualcóyotl Street, Cuernavaca, Morelos 62000

Location: Behind the cathedral, between Hidalgo and Abasolo Streets

Bob Brady, an American, left us this immensely charming legacy, a restored sixteenth-century house known as Casa de la Torre (House of the Tower). Touching the wall of the cathedral grounds, the house contains an eclectic collection of art and handcrafts, including works by Frida Kahlo and Milton Avery, while the garden features pre-Hispanic pieces. The sui generis style gives a sense of life in Cuernavaca of the 1960s and 1970s when Brady lived there.

Enclosed on either side by the tower and the cathedral wall, the central patio is a faithful imitation of Franciscan monastic gardens. A 100- or 200-year-old huamuchil (*Pithecellobium dulce*) presides over the patio like a living sculpture.

There are also fifteen different kinds of wild orchids, including *Epidendrum cebolleta, E. ibagense, E. nemorale, E. parkinsonianum, Cattleya* spp. Also, some *Gentianaceae, Helia alba, H. amoena,* and staghorn fern (*Platycerium bifurcatum*).

There is a cafeteria and gift shop, and space can be rented for special events.

Best time to visit: Year-round
Phone: (52) 73 18 85 54/14 35 29
Hours: 10–6 Tuesday–Sunday
E-mail: bradymus@mail.giga.com
Web site: geocities.com/thebradymuseum

## ETHNOBOTANICAL GARDEN AND MUSEUM OF TRADITIONAL MEDICINE/ HERBARIUM, INAH CENTER

14 Matamoros, Col. Acapatzingo,
Cuernavaca, Morelos 62440

Location: Follow Humboldt Street south from the center of Cuernavaca to its intersection with Rufino Tamayo Street, which enters from the left on the diagonal. Matamoros is the second street on the right past the intersection

Tradition has it that the El Olvido Ranch was bought in 1866 by Archduke Maximilian of Habsburg for one of his young lovers. It is four square hectares in area, with the Ethnobotanical Garden on the site of the former ranch and the museum located in the House of the India Bonita.

The museum is dedicated to the preservation of plants used in Mexican folk medicine over the centuries.

Best time to visit: Year-round
Phone: (52) 73 12 59 55/12 31 08/14 40 46
Hours: 10–4:30 daily
E-mail: cimor@mor1.telmex.net.mx

## SANTO DOMINGO ETHNOBOTANICAL MUSEUM AND CULTURAL CENTER

Reforma [unnumbered], between Constitución and Berriozábal, A.P. 367, Centro, Oaxaca, Oax. 68000

Location: Former convent of Santo Domingo

The flora of Oaxaca is the most diverse of all Mexico, calculated at more than 9,000 species of angiosperms (that is, flowering plants). Its unique botanical character reflects the high percentage of vegetation that is not native to any other part of the world.

The Ethnobotanical Garden is dedicated to the study and conservation of this plant diversity in its relationship to local culture. Founded in 1998, it includes a representa-tive selection of the state's various ecosystems and cultural heritages, located in the more than two square hectares of what was once the convent's orchard. As an ecological-cultural museum of Oaxaca's various ethnic groups, the garden uniquely complements the Museum of Culture and the Francisco de Burgoa Library. It also contains archaeological remains from the sixteenth and seventeenth centuries.

One of the plants represented here is the guaje (Leucaena esculenta), a relative of the bean family that is part of the Nahuatl name for the city: huaxácac, meaning "in the upper area of the guaje forest." The seeds, flowers, and buds of this plant are still part of the traditional diet in many regions of the state.

A member of the ceiba family, the coquito or shaving-brush tree (Pseudobombax ellipticum) is a spectacular plant often seen on the grounds of Oaxaca homes. Its bark is used in making rope and netting.

The economy of various extremely poor areas of the state depends on the soyate palm (Brahea dulcis). The palms are woven into hats, mats, baskets, and even toys.

The huixaco (Hechtia fragilis) belongs to the pine family. It grows in the dry lands of the Cuicatlán Cañada and Mixteca. Oaxaca contains the greatest number of varieties of this plant.

Best time to visit: Year-round
Phone: (52) 951 679 15/676 72
Hours: Guided tours 1–6 summer, 1–5 winter, Tuesday–Saturday
E-mail: Clarisaj@oaxaca.gob.mx

## MUSEUM AND EL LENCERO EX-HACIENDA

El Lencero, E. Zapata municipality, Veracruz, Ver. 91634

Location: Exit right from the Veracruz Highway 300 meters before the Campo Militar

In the patio at the back of the house, which is built on a naturally flat rock formation, there is an extraordinary 500-year-old fig tree nineteen meters in diameter. The ancient road leading up to the house has, on one side, a colonial chapel and restored rectory known as The House of the Nuns; on the other there are leafy Indian laurels (Nectandra ambigens) and yellow lilies (Merocalis livias). There is a little artesian-fed pond tucked away to the side, where swans swim peacefully. From the second story there is a view of the stately blue-and-green mountains that march endlessly along the horizon.

Founded in 1525, Lencero was one of the original eleven inns on the road from Veracruz to Mexico City. General Santa Anna bought the property in 1842, when it had 1,755 hectares. In addition to an inn, it has been a cattle ranch and a farm.

Best time to visit: Year-round
Phone: (52) 28 20 02 70
Admission: Free
Hours: 10–7 Tuesday–Sunday, winter 10–6 Tuesday–Sunday, summer

## XALAPA ANTHROPOLOGICAL MUSEUM

Corner of Av. Xalapa [unnumbered] and Acueducto, Xalapa 91010

Location: To the northeast of Xalapa, between Ave. 1 de Mayo and Acueducto

Founded in 1957, the Anthropological Museum of the City of Xalapa is one of the most important museums of its kind in Mexico. It offers magnificent examples of Gulf Coast archaeology in a natural setting that reproduces the jungle in which the pieces were originally found.

There are giant Olmec heads from southern Veracruz; also Oldham bamboos (Bambusa oldhamii), bird-of-paradise (Strelitzia reginae), jasmine (Gardenia jasminoides), and lollipops (Pachystachys lutea).

The museum was designed by the American architect Edward Durell Stone and the garden by landscape architect Alejandro Cabeza.

Best time to visit: Year-round
Phone: (52) 28 15 09 20
Hours: 9–5 daily
E-mail: museo@dino.coacade.uv.mx

## BOTANICAL GARDEN, FRANCISCO JAVIER CLAVIJERO ECOLOGICAL INSTITUTE

Km 2.5 mark on the old Coatepec Road, Xalapa, Veracruz 91000

Location: On the old Coatepec Road heading toward Briones

Xalapa de Enríquez, in Veracruz, is also called the City of Flowers. Its many parks and gardens give it one of the highest ratios of green space per capita of any Mexican city.

The Clavijero Botanical Garden was founded in 1977 on land once dedicated to the cultivation of coffee, citrus, and bananas. It sponsors research with an emphasis on protecting endangered local species. Popular with school groups, its eight hectares are divided into sections, most of which are connected by *tezontle* walkways. One of the most interesting sections is the mountainous forest crisscrossed by simple paths. Here one sees oaks and other trees and bushes typical of this climate, tree ferns, orchids, cacti, bromeliads, and aroids. Some of the trees shed their leaves in the winter only to break into many shades of green in the spring.

The arboretum's palm and pine collections include species from all over the world. A variety of local plants, both wild and cultivated, can be found in the medicinal herb garden, the formal garden, and around the pond. The Habitat I greenhouse features Mexican cycadas and plants from the warm, humid climate of southern Veracruz. Labels identify each plant's scientific name, popular name, habitat, and use.

The Mother Earth gift shop sells crafts reflective of Mexican conservation and management projects as well as plants and souvenirs.

Best time to visit: Year-round
Phone: (52) 28 42 18 27
Hours: 9–5 daily
E-mail: jbclavij@ecologia.edu.mx

## TEXCUTZINGO

Location: San Nicolás Tlaminca, 7 kilometers to the east of Texcoco City, Edo. de Mexico

Texcutzingo may well have been the first planned garden in the history of mankind: it is considered to be the most outstanding example of gardening and sustainable agriculture in the world.

The famous Texcutzingo Crag is a fifteenth-century archaeological site that contains the most fanciful gardens built by King Netzahualcóyotl of Texcoco. The structures known as the Netzahualcóyotl Baths are currently open to visitors, as well as some of the terraced fields, from which there is a magnificent view of the great Mexico valley. The area is also host to some of the more interesting and varied flora in the entire state. The visitor passes through a number of microclimates, with stands of tejocote, apple, and nopales, scrub forests, groves, and fields.

Best time to visit: During the rainy season (May–September), when the flowers are most abundant

Index

## PHOTO CREDITS

Guillermo Aldana
2–3, 4, 7, 8, 24, 28–29, 32–33, 34 *(above right, below left)*, 36 *(above right, below right)*, 37, 38 *(1, 4)*, 39, 40 *(above)*, 41 *(above right)*, 42–43, 46–47, 50 *(1)*, 51 *(3, 7)*, 52 *(below)*, 54–55, 64, 65, 66–67, 86, 87, 88–89, 90, 92–93, 94, 95, 96, 97, 98–99, 100, 101, 102–3, 104, 105, 106, 107, 108, 109, 110, 111, 112–13, 130, 146, 147, 148–49, 150, 151, 152–53, 218, 219, 220, 221, 228 *(above middle, below middle)*

Laura Cohen
171 *(right)*, 172 *(above left, left, below right)*, 173 *(below)*

Gabriel Figueroa Flores
35, 40 *(below)*, 50 *(2)*, 51 *(5)*, 60, 61, 82, 83, 84–85, 114, 116–17, 118, 119, 121 *(left)*, 122, 123, 124, 126, 127, 128–29, 135, 136, 137, 138, 139, 140, 160, 161, 168, 169

Eric Giebeler
180, 181 *(below left)*, 182–83

Amanda Holmes
222, 223, 224, 225, 226–27

Juan Pintor
51 *(4)*

Armando Salas Portugal
17

Bob Schalkwijk
1, 23, 30, 36 *(above left)*, 38 *(2, 5)*, 41 *(above left)*, 44, 48 *(below left)*, 49, 51 *(6)*, 52 *(above)*, 53, 56, 62, 63, 68, 69, 70, 71, 72–73, 74, 75, 76, 77, 78, 79, 80, 81, 120, 121 *(right)*, 125, 132–33, 140, 141, 142, 143, 144–45, 154, 156–57, 162, 163, 164–65, 166, 167, 174, 176–77, 178, 179, 181 *(above left, above right)*, 184, 185, 186–87, 188, 189, 190–91, 192, 193, 194, 195, 196–97, 198, 199, 200, 201, 202, 203, 204, 208, 209, 216, 217, 228 *(above left, above right, middle left, middle, middle right, below left, below right)*, 236

Pim Schalkwijk
58–59

Personal Archive: Guillermo Tovar y de Teresa
10, 12–13, 14

Ignacio Urquiza
18, 19, 34 *(above left, below right)*, 38 *(3)*, 41 *(below left)*, 48 *(above, below right)*, 158, 159, 170, 171 *(left)*, 172 *(above right)*, 173 *(above)*, 206–7, 210, 211, 212, 213, 214, 215

Alejandra Villela
134